The Theater of Healing

American University Studies

Series XXVI
Theatre Arts

Vol. 24

PETER LANG
New York • Washington, D.C./Baltimore • San Francisco
Bern • Frankfurt am Main • Berlin • Vienna • Paris

E. D. Karampetsos

The Theater of Healing

PETER LANG
New York • Washington, D.C./Baltimore • San Francisco
Bern • Frankfurt am Main • Berlin • Vienna • Paris

Library of Congress Cataloging-in-Publication Data

Karampetsos, E. D.
The theater of healing/ E. D. Karampetsos.
    p.   cm.—(American university studies. Series XXVI, Theatre arts;
vol. 24)
    Includes bibliographical references and index.
    1. Drama—20th century—History and criticism. 2. Myth in literature.
I. Title. II. Series.
PN1861.K353   809.2'04—dc20   94–36638
ISBN 0-8204-2651-2
ISSN 0899-9880

Die Deutsche Bibliothek—CIP—Einheitsaufnahme

Karampetsos, E. D.
The theater of healing/ E. D. Karampetsos. - New York; Washington,
D.C./Baltimore; San Francisco; Bern; Frankfurt am Main; Berlin; Vienna;
Paris: Lang.
    (American university studies. Series 26, Theatre arts; vol. 24)
    ISBN 0-8204-2651-2
NE: GT

The paper in this book meets the guidelines for permanence and durability
of the Committee on Production Guidelines for Book Longevity of the
Council of Library Resources.

Printed in the United States of America.

for Sotiroulla

Acknowledgments

Several acknowledgments are in order. To Lillian Feder, Rosette Lamont, Daniel Gerould and Burton Pike, the members of my dissertation committee, who supervised the original draft of this book. To Michael Mitias who encouraged me to continue my research and to find a publisher for my work. To Piers Smith, Kenneth Payne, Madeline Haggan and Reid Maynard, my colleagues at Kuwait University, and A. C. Nunn whose corrections and suggestions helped make *The Theater of Healing* a much better book. To Alan Balboni, Marion Martin and Dorothy Gregory who supplied me with reference materials from afar. To my wife Sotiroulla, who has been my in-house critic and constant source of inspiration.

Table of Contents

Chapter One

The Theater of Healing

As Nietzsche pointed out in *The Birth of Tragedy*, the audience of today, like that of the ancient Greeks, awaits the coming of the tragic figure to behold not "the awkwardly masked man but a figure born of their own rapt vision" (58). Nietzsche's poetic vision of a metaphysical theater capable of healing the existential problems of his time helped provoke a revolution in Western drama. Playwrights were inspired to write plays about the audience, about its problems, hopes and fears. Yeats, Artaud, Brecht, Genet, Ionesco and others found ways to present the abstract forces of modern society in a form which permits the spectator to contemplate and find ways to master them. Exploiting the revolutionary changes taking place in Western theater, they borrowed freely from opera and ballet, scrutinized accounts of myth and ritual in traditional societies for elements they could reclaim, and they ransacked the theater traditions of other cultures, especially of Asia, for ideas and models which they could use in the creation of a new kind of theater. While studying about artists in traditional societies, such as the shaman, who combined the roles of poet and dramatist with those of spiritual healer and leader, playwrights began to imagine themselves assuming similar functions. The West, as Nietzsche had argued, was in crisis, why should not art replace those institutions which had failed? If society had become disoriented and a source of alienation for the individual, the solution was to create new myths and rituals appropriate to the needs of their audience. Thus, as Nietzsche had hoped, in the creation of a theater of healing, a way was found for the modern audience to rediscover the ability of the ancient Greeks to contemplate their gods and, having seen them, challenge them.

In the process of creating metaphysical theater the use of traditional myths, particularly those of Greece and Rome, was rejected, because it was felt that they had lost their original importance as sources of metaphysical knowledge, and had been reduced to objects of intellectual contemplation for the cultured few. Treating Nietzsche's metaphor of the library of Alexandria, smothered by scholarly glosses and the dust of centuries, as Alexander the Great did the Gordian Knot, Artaud proclaimed burning the library to the ground as the only solution, for only what is essential, necessary, and truly vital would survive (IV, 15). Unlike those who turn to classical myths for a decor, a plot, or merely to give their work a sense of profundity, in metaphysical theater we find a search for something far more vital: a story and a form of presentation with metaphysical significance for our own times. The gods and heroes of classical myth have been replaced by a more contemporary vision of the forces which govern our lives. Instead of anthropomorphic gods, they bring to the stage images of man-made forces (economic, political, technological, and social) grown to superhuman proportions and, out of control, turning their power on their makers.

There is no all-inclusive definition of ritual and myth, but in general these are their characteristics and objectives which are found in the theater of healing: 1) myth must express the contemporary experience of man and not merely be an imitation or borrowing from the myths of another time or culture; 2) the mythical play has a metaphysical dimension which gives substance to forces and situations whose nature is otherwise abstract and insubstantial; 3) an objective of mythical drama is to present an image of the human situation, not a realistic picture of the solitary individual in a particular situation; 4) the mythical characters and situations are archetypal representations of the forces which the playwright perceives as governing the world; the actions of the characters are often ritual in the sense that they have an inevitability associated with them which predetermines their behavior and the outcome of the situations; and 5) there is the use of ritual techniques as a means of giving concrete form to the metaphysical and of emphasizing the archetypal nature of the characters and situations in the plays—a means of revealing the differences between freely chosen actions and forms of behavior which have encrusted themselves on life. In addition, the use of ritual is related to a concern for the totality of effect of the plays, a desire to affect both the intellect and the emotions.

A variety of factors, many of them unrelated to Nietzsche's theories, made possible and contributed to the creation of a metaphysical theater. Our ideas about the nature of art, of what it is and how it works its effect, were transformed by Kant, Freud and others. There was also the feeling that Western theater had reached an impasse, that it either had to renew itself or be abandoned. At the same time, contact with theater traditions of cultures outside the West demonstrated a seemingly infinite variety of possibilities for renewing the theater. Late nineteenth century anthropological studies inspired artists to believe that ancient myth and ritual possessed neglected primitive powers just waiting to be unleashed by art. Of the various experiments with new theatrical forms, metaphysical theater has been one of the most innovative and ambitious.

In a discussion of theater and myth it is almost impossible to avoid the word "ritual." Unfortunately, it has so many definitions that its use often contributes more confusion than clarity. It is associated with primitive, pre-verbal forms of expression. Some see it as the acted correlative of myth. Ritual is associated with the Eastern Orthodox liturgy and the Roman Catholic mass where it has something to do with candlelight, chanting, the sound of swinging thuribles and the smell of incense. Unfortunately it is impossible to avoid it or to think of a better word to replace it; thus I wish to propose here a very limited definition of ritual related to its function in the theater of healing.

First of all, ritual is a means of behavior, of body movement, which replaces realistic acting. Instead of feigning natural behavior, the actor uses ritual movement to call attention to the artifice of the play. Brecht called upon actors to destroy the illusion of realism by making it obvious that they were acting. One of the objectives of using ritual is to thwart the tendency to identify with a character or with the actor. Artaud, Yeats, and Brecht borrowed techniques from the Japanese Noh theater which they felt would emphasize the distinction between the actor and the action being performed.

Theoretically, ritual is also a means of manipulating the psychic distance between the spectator and the performance. The idea of some sort of inviolable and immutable esthetic distance is replaced with a potentially infinite variety of distances. One moment the spectator can be treated like an observer in a lecture hall, or at a rehearsal, and the next plunged into emotional participation in the action on-stage. The first time I experienced such a use of ritual was in 1964 when I attended a performance of Luigi Pirandello's *Tonight We Improvise* in Athens. In one scene the actor rehearses the act of dying, which is followed by the death of the character. In spite of, or possibly because of, Pirandello's destruction of the illusion of theatrical reality, I found myself no longer watching a death scene, but inescapably involved in the experience of death.[1]

A second use for ritual is as a gauge, or indicator, of psychic reality. It is a means of calling attention to the discrepancy between that which is authentic and that which is not. Here, for example, I think of the installation scene of Cardinal Barberini in Brecht's *Galileo* and Genet's costuming scenes in *The Balcony*. In both plays as the characters put on their costumes there is a

---

[1] Of the same scene in Pirandello's *Tonight We Improvise*, Lionel Abel writes: "Pirandello is able to touch us with the feeling of the real imminence of death in a way he would never have been able to do by showing us a man really dying" (80).

metaphysical revelation of the difference between their humanity and the inhumanity of the roles they are about to assume.

Finally, ritual is a means of involving the spectator in the creation of the play. Alone, ritual is wordless. It can also accompany words intended to be understood not literally, but on an emotional level. Where the emotions generated by the play are strong enough, the ritual serves as a sign without signification and provokes the participation of the spectator in establishing the significance of the scene.

Ritual grows out of and is the expression of a mode of perception whose function is to bring the inner self of the individual into harmony with the universe. It draws our attention to the essence of human experience while sloughing off superfluous and distracting phenomena. In ritual, experience becomes unified and coherent. Although we often associate ritual with primitive societies and its occasional manifestations in the theater and secret societies, it is inescapably part of our way of understanding and acting in the world.

Ritual, according to Suzanne K. Langer, precedes symbolism, language and, therefore, the possibility of meaning. Ritual, she says, is a response to basic human needs which, although neglected, lie at the origin of human consciousness and which continue to exist. Ritual, like the empirical quest for knowledge, is an integral part of "the **human response**, as a constructive, not a passive thing" (24). It is constructive because it leads to the creation of symbolism, language and art. This response arises from the compulsive need of the inner self to establish contact with the outer self. The original creative response of the primitive person, Langer tells us, initiated a process of continuing self-creation which continues until today.

Some playwrights, such as Antonin Artaud and W. B. Yeats, expected almost miraculous results from their use of myth and ritual and, inevitably, they were disappointed. If Yeats and Artaud failed to return to the theater its sacred and healing role, if they failed to create a new priesthood of artists and a growing congregation of believers, it is perhaps because, as Ionesco has said of Artaud, they were neither gods nor demons ("Ni" 24). Nevertheless, they have transformed modern drama. They have restored its tragic vision. They have reminded playwrights that the vast estate of the theater contains elements of the sacred, the ability to give concrete expression to our metaphysical thoughts, to create new myths and rituals for our time, and to restore value and meaning to an absurd universe.

Contrary to those who argued that the individual cannot be changed until society changes, those who created the theater of healing felt that first the individual must change—it is necessary to become aware of one's unconscious needs and desires. And before society or the individual can be changed, we must first imagine a new order. According to Hans Robert Jauss, such a transformation constitutes a form of catharsis. "One of the functions of art," says Jauss, is "to discover new modes of experience in a changing reality or to propose alternatives to it" (63). Art must involve the spectator, he argues, as "an active participant in the constitution of the imaginary" (92). Health is the product of a liberated imagination which "stirred by affects and set free, can act" (96).

The healthy, essential relationship between the theater and the spectator, as Artaud described it, is one which attacks and destroys the masks and lies which separate us from a true knowledge of ourselves and the meaning of life. Speaking of his vision of a new, healing theater of myth and ritual, Artaud claimed "It knocks off the mask; it discovers lies, emptiness, baseness, hypocrisy." He imagined that revelation of the metaphysical realities of life would invite the members of the audience "to take a heroic and superior stance which they had never before possessed" (IV, 147).

The need to return the theater to its ancient sources in the rites of Dionysus was set forth by Nietzsche in *The Birth of Tragedy*. Only a restoration of the "tragic vision" of the ancient Greeks, he argued, could heal the soul of modern man and lead to a higher form of nihilism which, without denying the absurdity of existence, would bring us to the edge of the abyss. The tragic vision would teach us to live with these cruel realities and renew our love of life while, at the same time, providing it with an ethical basis.

We are all familiar with Nietzsche's argument that Christianity and Socrates (with the help of Euripides) are responsible for the spiritual malaise of modern man; that our institutions, founded on the Socratic faith in science and progress, have left us in the deadening grip of the Apollonian; and that only the return of the Dionysian can restore to us the healing power of the tragic vision. The Dionysian, using Apollonian artifice, brings the individual into a salutary confrontation with death. "Then," according to Nietzsche, "it becomes evident that the poet's whole conception is nothing but precisely that bright image which healing nature projects before us after a glance into the abyss" (68). The Dionysian, Nietzsche explained, addresses itself to the great enemy of death, the libido, *Eros*: "The metaphysical solace (with which, I wish to say at once, all true tragedy sends us away) that, despite every phenomenal change, life is at bottom indestructibly joyful and powerful" (50). Poetry, if it is to demonstrate its faith in humanity, can no longer be concerned with reflecting "the supposed reality of civilized man." What Nietzsche proposed is no less than an art form which can force us to recognize "the eternal core of things" behind the socially and culturally imposed mask, which we are accustomed to accepting as the face of reality. He wanted theater to help us rediscover our authentic selves, "to the eternity of true being surviving every phenomenal change" (53).

In the fifth century, when they attempted to rationalize a mythology that was clearly at variance with their religious and ethical sensibilities, the Greeks faced a dilemma similar to the one described by Nietzsche. The stories handed down about the gods were all too often at variance with the prevailing ethical and philosophical values of the Greeks.

Over the centuries Greek mythology accumulated incongruous, often incompatible, stories about their gods and heroes. These contradictions reflected stages in the development of Greek religious thought as well as local permutations of panhellenic myths. An example of the problems they faced is found in J. E. Harrison's discussion of the different forms of Dionysus. There was never a single Dionysus, but a god always in the process of becoming that which the ancient religious imagination was capable of seeing in him. At different stages Dionysus was phytomorphic, zoomorphic and anthropomorphic, and within these categories he was attributed many more identities.

Contemporaries of Plutarch, such as Socrates and Plato, looking for the true and the ideal, came to the conclusion that the gods of their ancestors were no longer convenient or credible. They felt compelled to choose: they could deny some of the identities and profess an uneasy faith in what they had chosen to believe, or, they could build a monument to the unknown god and wait. The rational analysis of the philosophers did not provide the final answer, because the Greeks were unwilling to discard their ancient heritage. By drawing the subject matter of their plays from Greek mythology, Athenian dramatists demonstrated that, although the stories told about the gods might not be factually true, the truth they contained was still valid. These plays, as Nietzsche realized, demonstrated that the theater should not submit to the demands of logic: Dionysus and his many identities are not the truth, but proof of a human impulse to reify, through art, its metaphysical concerns as a means of giving expression to our ever-evolving human identity. The mistake of the ancients, as Nietzsche saw it, was to assume that at one point or another this becoming would end, that a particular symbol, or collection of symbols, could somehow be the permanent repository of truth. The truth, however, as Nietzsche argued, is ephemeral; it exists for a moment when the Dionysian meets the Apollonian. In other words, the symbol and the meaning ascribed to it are not permanent and the difference between them grows from the moment the symbol comes into existence (Thiher 503).

Whereas Nietzsche directed our attention to the role of the artist in giving expression to our metaphysical concerns, Kant set aside the Platonic theory that art is only an imitation of reality. As Albert Hofstadter points out, after Kant, and those who, like Schopenhauer and Schelling developed Kantian idealism, it became clear that the only way to know reality, or the world of ideas, was through art: "art and aesthetic intuition became the organ by which the philosopher could achieve ultimate insight into the nature of reality" (4). The work of art is no longer seen as an imitation of the material world of appearances, but is the concretization of a poetic intuition of the world of ideas. Instead of being thrice removed from ideal truth, as Plato would have it, the work of art is as close as we can come to knowing the truth.

Art makes concrete our metaphysical concerns. The act of creation is both revolutionary and conservative. Truth exists as an intuition, a sentiment, and the artist gives it concrete existence in the form of a work of art. Its truth is verified by the audience, which recognizes in it the shared, but hitherto unexpressed, idea. Art is revolutionary because the act of creation redefines and alters man's relation to himself and the world. It is conservative because the artistic image, once completed, gives the illusion that no more can be said, that the illusion and the truth are the one and eternal (Rank 123). Once completed, the image created by the artist becomes part of the public domain; it can be appropriated by religion to represent its truths and to fix them for eternity, as perfect and unalterable as the marbles of Praxiteles or Phedias.

Humanity and its environment, however, are dynamic and the fixed forms of traditional art, the works we often describe as classics, cannot permanently explain man's status in an ever-changing universe. Religions may lose their relevance or die out, philosophical ideas and scientific theories may succeed one another, but when the objects of faith become inadequate, some people, unwilling to accept the idea of a universe in constant flux, compensate for their insecurity by clinging ever more tightly to those symbols which once represented the truth, while others surrender to the despair, the nihilism, the sense of absurdity, that accompanies the loss of belief. If we accept the idea that the symbols by which we live represent only elusive truths, as ephemeral and transient as the world we live in, then it stands to reason that the pursuit of truth can never end or be satisfied even with the most beautiful creations. Instead of insisting on preserving a static, false vision of life, we must, as Nietzsche argued, be prepared to embrace change, to accept the idea of becoming (Del Caro 18-19).

We must, therefore, regain the tragic vision which expresses the metaphysical truths essential to a healthy spiritual life. To accomplish Nietzsche's program, it would be necessary for the artist to recombine, as they once were, in our very ancient past, the roles of poet, priest, dramatist, mystic, and leader of souls in a single person. This was an argument for a humanist religion, an impossible project, which presupposed the existence of an audience willing to accept a situation in which its most cherished beliefs and illusions are constantly challenged. It was a call for a dynamic form of theater which rejects surface permanence as part of a continuing search for metaphysical truth.

Later in his career, as his ideas evolved, Nietzsche put behind him his concerns with metaphysics, the theater, and art as the source of metaphysical regeneration. Dionysus, as Del Caro notes, became a philosopher, because Nietzsche felt the Apollonian would undermine his Dionysian aesthetics. The danger of collaboration with the Apollonian, as suggested above, is that the work of art, i.e., that concrete form in which the tragic vision of Dionysus briefly manifests itself, ultimately serves to support the conservative, static anti-life forces. It is this danger which led Nietzsche, in his later works, to reject the metaphysical vision, to reject cooperation with the Apollonian (Del Caro 45, 52, 54, 105).

Though Nietzsche abandoned the idea of a metaphysical theater, others, taking up the challenge of creating a dynamic, permanently changing theater, went on to incorporate his ideas in their research and in their plays. After all, is there an art form better suited to the conjuration of this transitory vision of man's tragic reality than the theater? Here, as Artaud reminded us, we must not think in terms of plays, of literary masterpieces, but of the performance in which the play is only a minor part. Unlike the marble statues and the oil paintings with their illusion of permanence, in the theater the work of art does not survive the performance. On the stage, the Dionysian calls upon the Apollonian for its most limited and ephemeral cooperation. It is up to the people of the theater to ensure that its dynamism is maintained.

Among those who envisioned a new form of drama was Mallarmé. Inspired by the operas of Wagner and by the ballet, he dreamt of a new, symbolist theater which would use all of the arts at its disposal. Mallarmé's work in the theater reflects the development of a new sensibility in the late nineteenth century which demanded the return of Dionysus.

The realistic stage sets and the histrionics typical of the Parisian stage in the late nineteenth century repelled Mallarmé and his fellow symbolists. Recalling Aristotle, who preferred poetry to history, because it is "a more philosophical and higher thing" (ix 3), Mallarmé condemned realistic drama for presenting voyeuristic slices of life about other people whom one watches merely out of curiosity and without the possibility of finding in the performance a reflection of one's own reality. Drama, he argued, should concern itself primarily with the spectator, about the tragic truth of the human condition: "the antagonism in man between the dream and the fatalities in his existence meted out by misfortune" (300).

The creation of a new theater, as Mallarmé imagined it, would have required a complete reconsideration of the nature of drama. "Replace vaudeville with mystery" (313) best describes what he and, after him, Artaud had in mind: a return to the sacred mysteries of Dionysus—mysteries which reveal the secrets of the universe; mysteries which demystify. "In this sense," as Haskell Block points out, "Mallarmé's ritual drama is the means of the propagation of a new religion, a secularization of the liturgy and rite of ancient dramatic performances" (85).

Weary of the bombast and the dreary realism of the late nineteenth-century stage, Mallarmé wanted to purify the language of the theater, to make it emblematic. Although he has not left us a precise definition of the theater he imagined, Mallarmé provided us with several hints of what some of its traits should be. In the ballet, he found a divine vision worthy of replacing "the monster . . . which struts in the sacred space" (313); he anticipated Artaud's concept of a concrete language when he read in the dancer's movement "physical writing which would require paragraphs to express . . ." (304). For example, he envied the ability of dance to transform the dancer into "a metaphor epitomizing in the elementary aspects of our shape, sword, cup, flower" (304). Mallarmé wished the theater could be redeemed as it was, for a single moment, in a performance of *Hamlet*, by "the exorcism of a gesture" (302). In his desire to communicate symbolically, by means of gesture, he imagined a situation in which the audience participates in creating a play, because it has to read the gesture and give it meaning. In the works of Wagner, Mallarmé recognized the possibility of uniting the symbolic elements of drama into a total poetic unity (323-324). Instead of richly upholstered and cluttered stage sets, Mallarmé called for a restraint and perfection which "neither hinders nor conceals the future" (316).

Mallarmé imagined the stage without its clutter, but he doubted the ability of the theater to escape the tyranny of the word, because, despite his dream of an ideal drama, he considered theater in essence to be, literature best realized in the theater of the mind where its poetry could be expressed in its fullest, most emblematic manner.

Mallarmé's own efforts at playwriting, *L'Après-midi d'un Faune* and *Hérodiade*, never came to fruition, partially because he felt they would never find a place in the commercial theater and because of his conviction that the only proper stage is the mind. Perhaps Mallarmé was closer to accomplishing his objectives than he suspected. His ideas found expression on the stage in the works of other playwrights. Even his choice of subject for *Hérodiade*, the story of Salomé, shows that Mallarmé knew what would fascinate his contemporaries. As Wayne K. Chapman points out, "a veritable cult of Salomé existed in the nineties . . . celebrated in the pictures of Moreau and Beardsley, in Wilde's play, and several of Symons's . . . poems" (20). Mallarmé, and later Yeats, chose the dance of Salomé and the beheading of John the Baptist, because its motifs symbolize the Nietzschean *amor fati*, the fatal meeting between *eros* and *thanatos*.

Mallarmé's ideas led his fellow symbolists and disciples to give substance to the theater of his dreams. His influence can be found in the symbolist plays of Maurice Maeterlinck, Paul Claudel, Henri de Régnier, Emile Verhaeren, Francis Vielé-Griffin and others. Unfortunately, the symbolists were not very good as dramatists and their plays are virtually ignored today. Instead, Alfred Jarry's *Ubu Roi* won the honor for being one of the first great modern plays.

Jarry had been a close associate of the symbolists; he attended Mallarmé's *mardis* and wrote symbolist poetry, but when it came to theater his idiosyncratic interpretation of the world and the lessons of symbolism led to something quite unexpected. Keeping in mind Mallarmé's preference for the more refined arts (ballet, the operas of Wagner, *Hamlet*) and his lofty dreams for humanity, it may come almost as a surprise that he recognized his ideas manifested in the guise of Jarry's play. Jarry's puppet show for adults is far from the delicate sensibility, the immaculate *azure*, associated with the poetry of Mallarmé; but, like the arrival of Dionysus in the kingdom of Cadmus, it signaled the arrival of a disturbing and revolutionary force in European theater.

First performed in 1896, Jarry's play caused a scandal. Jarry's protagonists, the pear-shaped Ubu and his wife, are emblematic of humanity's worst instincts: cowardice, treachery, avarice, lust, homicide. The treatment of the characters is symbolic, as Keith Beaumont writes, they are ciphers upon which "the audience is implicitly invited to actively project its own 'meaning' or interpretation into the abstract or semi-abstract framework created by the playwright" (112). The characters are puppets, inspired by the *guignol* of Jarry's youth, in human bodies dressed for a children's masquerade. The armies of Poland and Russia are represented by one toy soldier each and their battles are on the level of nursery-school make-believe. The cruel traits of Jarry's characters replaced the detailed case histories of the realist theater with abstract, mythological beings whose actions give expression to the tragic history of all mankind.

More important than Jarry's themes is his revolutionary attack on the realistic theater of the time. Here, in the boldest terms possible, was a new way of conceiving of the theater, one clearly influenced by the symbolists. The puppet-like behavior of Jarry's characters fulfills the function intended by the symbolists: it draws attention to the artifice and away from the individual actor; anti-mimetic, it breaks the connection between the actor/character and any realistic significance the role might contain, obliging the spectator to find meaning on a metaphysical level. More important, perhaps, Jarry realized that to create metaphysical theater, it was not necessary to turn to ancient myth and legends. It was enough to perceive the abstract, universal human reality beneath the surface reality of everyday life and to bring that to the stage.

The revolutionary value of the play was recognized by Mallarmé who praised its author for creating a character who "enters the repertoire of high taste and haunts me" (qtd. in

Beaumont 115). Yeats, who was also in the audience, applauded with Jarry's partisans, although, as he noted in *The Autobiographies*, not without a sense of trepidation as to what *Ubu Roi* presaged for the arts:

> After Stéphane Mallarmé, after Paul Verlaine, after Gustav Moreau, after Puvis de Chavannes, after our own verse, after all our subtle color and nervous rhythm, after the faint tints of Conder, what more is possible? After us, the Savage God" (233-234).

It was up to Jarry's successors to struggle with the Savage God.

Yeats may have served a different god (or gods and demons), but his plays grew out of dramatic principles not unlike those which inspired Jarry's work. But, because Yeats was one of the first to pull together enough of the theories about the new theater to create something original in content and form, while, at the same time, doing it with metaphysical objectives in mind, I present him here as the first of the modern shamans.

In many ways, Yeats conceived of his mission as a poet and dramatist not as an end, but as a means of attaining spiritual, ethnic, and revolutionary goals. Yeats imagined the poet as a priest and leader of souls, as is evidenced in his essay "The Body of the Father Christian Rosencrux," where he wrote, "this age of criticism is about to pass, and an age of imagination, of emotion, of moods, of revelation, about to come in its place; for certainly belief in a supersensual world is at hand again" (EI 197).

In what we might today describe as a postcolonial project, Yeats and his colleagues wanted to create an Irish literature as distinct from that of the English. Yeats had a vision of leading his countrymen in the establishment of a spiritually reinvigorated Ireland and he intended to use the theater as a means of attaining his objectives. Yeats's objective, according to Morton Seiden, was to recover his people's Irish identity, and this, he felt, would lead, in each individual, to a recognition of one's authentic self, to the emotional fullness which must precede intellectual and physical action. Yeats wanted "to define and evoke the whole realm of psychic vision, to render that vision paradoxically in both literal and metaphysical language" (287). Drama, not poetry, Yeats felt, was the proper vehicle for such a program, because it brings people together in a liturgical experience and contributes to the communal feelings needed for national unity.

More concretely, his activities were directed toward the establishment of an Irish mystical order and an Irish theater. The order was to provide a basis for literary work directed at the Irish masses. In "Ireland and the Arts" (1904), Yeats maintained that the artist's duty was not to entertain "a few people who have grown up in a leisured class and make this understanding their business." The artist must become a missionary to an entire nation and use his art to free those shackled by mundane concerns (EI 203, 206).

At first, Yeats was primarily concerned with the content of his plays; the discovery of a form of theater befitting his vision came later and gradually. *The Countess Cathleen* (1889-1890) and *The Land of the Heart's Desire* (1894), his first plays, were from Yeats's point of view, mystery or miracle plays which revealed, not Christian truth, but the spiritual world of Irish myth and tradition. That invisible world, if Yeats's hopes could have been realized, would have become a metaphysical source of strength for the Irish national movement, because it would have led the Irish to set aside their personal interests in deference to a common ethnic bond (Ellman 115-134).

Yeats understood that the invisible world of the Irishman was inaccessible to logic or empirical demonstration: instead it had to be reached by an act of faith through mystical union with a collective will. The artist's materials are not possessions of the church, but the living tales of Cuchulain, Emer and Conchubar— accounts of life and death, great battles which included spirits and mortals, great loves and equally great deprivations.

Yeats took from the Irish their myths and legends and returned them in a form enhanced by art. The renewed mythology, he hoped, would bring with it the freedom to indulge in the physical joys of life with the knowing and willing concurrence of the mind. It would be a new weapon to cut through the pettiness and narrow-mindedness of poverty and servitude. "We were to forge in Ireland," Yeats says in "Poverty and Tradition" (1910), "a new sword on our old traditional anvil for that great battle that must in the end re-establish the old confident, joyous world" (EI 249). Unfortunately for Yeats, his first plays did not bring about the hoped for mystical union of the audience. Spectators simply did not respond as he had intended. Yeats faced the same problem Artaud and Brecht would encounter later: the virtual impossibility for a play, or even several plays, to transform society, to change people's lives or beliefs.

In 1916, setting aside his desire to move an entire nation, Yeats came under the influence of the Japanese Noh theater, which profoundly influenced his approach to myth and theater. Although Yeats had long known the ritual connotations of theater, the potential in his plays for dance, of ritual movement, became clear to him on seeing a performance of the Japanese dancer Mr. Ito. In a small, simple hall, with neither decoration nor special stage lighting, the mere movements of Mr. Ito's body were a revelation. He seemed "to recede from us into some more powerful life. Because that separation was achieved by human means alone, he receded but to inhabit as it were the deeps of the mind." Yeats discovered that the strength of the emotion is stronger because the gesture is vague and is perceived on the affective level where its truth is immediately recognized without the mediation of the conscious intellect. "We only believe in those thoughts which have been conceived not in the brain but in the whole body." Here, Yeats proposed a means of achieving the Nietzschean ideal. "The end of art," he said, "is the ecstasy awakened by the presence before an ever-changing mind of what is permanent in the world" (EI 287).

Ezra Pound, who, at the same time, was completing the translations of Noh plays and the introduction to them left unfinished by Ernest Fenollosa, enlarged Yeats's knowledge of oriental drama by introducing him to Noh theater. From Pound he learned that the plots of the Noh theater are founded on myths expressed in a combination of dance, gesture, chanting and minimal scenic effects. Here was exactly what Yeats had been looking for, an anti-mimetic theater that was the polar opposite of the naturalist drama which dominated the European stage of the late nineteenth century.

Critics have pointed out that Yeats's contact with the Noh theater was not ideal.[2] However, the point here is not that Yeats wanted to import the Noh theater to Ireland and the rest of Europe, but that he found an existing form of drama that successfully combined many of the elements with which he and the symbolists had been experimenting. It helped him to go beyond certain conceptual barriers inherited from the ancient Greeks. Aristotle admits the "emotional attraction" of spectacle, but, at the same time, dismisses it as the "least artistic" element of the art of poetry, a preference which became standard in Western theater (VI, 1450b). Oriental theater, by contrast, gives greater emphasis to the spectacle and, consequently, has formed and relies on an audience which possesses a heightened sensibility for the subtleties of gesture and symbol. Above all, what Yeats and other western dramatists who looked to oriental drama for ideas and inspiration found was proof of the polymorphous potential of theater.

Yeats had no intention of becoming an Irish Zeami; instead he turned to Asia, as he did to continental Europe, both as an artist and as a nationalist, seeking materials to embody his vision.

---

[2] According to Daniel Albright, Mr. Ito learned dance from Eugene Dalacroze, not in Japan (36). Albright dismisses Yeats' ideas about the Noh theater as "exhuberant fantasies bred in considerable ignorance" (34). In a similar manner, Steven Putzel explains that Yeats, though he had access to only fragments of Zeami's esthetics, seems to have discovered many of the Japanese playwright's ideas as he imitated his plays: "The concept of aesthetic distance, stylized movement and dance, stasis, the primary (sic) of poetry over action, and the function of the chorus" (109).

We are fortunate that Yeats, like Artaud, Brecht and others, approached oriental theater not as academics striving for some ideal understanding but as artists seeking ideas and inspiration for their own work, because they produced living drama and not more of the museum pieces they hated.

Regardless of the quality of Mr. Ito's performance and Yeats's own research into the Noh, Yeats already had the example of Mallarmé's *Hérodiade* and the taste of his time to guide him in the use of the dancer. The dance, the dropping of the veil, the severed–head, motifs of the story of Salomé, recur in Yeats's Noh plays *A Full Moon in March* and *The Death of Cuchulain*. These are the elements of "a dramatic situation" which, as Chapman observes, "he used repeatedly to dramatize the moment of tragic joy: the dance represents the poetic illumination of the soul at its zero moment, when the soul simultaneously meets death and trades her mortal dream for a consummation with eternal reality" (24).

Yeats's Noh plays are simple, direct and very moving. Yeats claimed to have "invented a form of drama, distinguished, indirect, and symbolic, having no need of mob or Press to pay its way—an aristocratic form" (EI 221). He had found a way to express the metaphysical truths of his time and people. Inadvertently, in developing a ritual form of theater to complement his Dionysian themes, Yeats created a popular form of drama worthy of comparison with the best work of this century.

Yeats's efforts to create a theater of myth and ritual were renewed by Artaud who worked for a new form of drama with, according to Ionesco, "an unbounded messianic ambition." Like Yeats, his expectations have to be measured against the reality of an audience which, although it could appreciate his theatrical innovations, did not necessarily share his faith in the redemptive powers of myth and ritual. As Ionesco has remarked, "his flaw wasn't that he was merely a poet or a dramatist, but neither a god nor a demon; just an actor and producer, or rather stage manager" ("Ni": 24).

Artaud's hypersensitivity to myth and ritual is attributed by Bettina Knapp to his unstable mental condition and the severe migraines which plagued him all his life. This "led him to opt for a theater which worked on the nerves and the senses, and reject one which sought to speak to the intellect" (45). Yet, as we have seen in the cases of Yeats, Mallarmé, and the young Nietzsche, it is not necessary to be mad to want to bypass the intellect in order to speak directly to the audience on the level of the emotions. At worst, Artaud's psychological problems can be blamed for no more than reinforcing his faith in the theater of myth and ritual.

Why would an audience take Artaud's objectives seriously? Or those of Yeats? In their enthusiasm for myth and ritual, they were reacting positively to some of the best scientific thinking of their time: to the work on myth and ritual of the Cambridge anthropologists (such as Frazer's *Golden Bough*), to Freud, Jung, Rank and others. If Yeats and Artaud were alive today, they might find inspiration, for example, in the work of Eliade, Levi Strauss, Rollo May, J. L. Moreno's research in psychodrama, in the theories of the structuralist, semiological, and deconstructivist critics, and many others who have explored the ways in which our physical and spiritual health are affected because we read the world like a text which contains both literal, surface meaning and connotations, often barely perceived by the conscious mind.

We should not be surprised to read about Artaud studying psychology and anthropology one moment, and the next, running to the New World in search of the secrets of the Tupamaras and to the Balinese theater for lessons on the proper use of myth and ritual. (After all, Nietzsche might not have sought to revive the atavistic powers of the pre-Socratic Dionysus had there not been a widely accepted Western tradition, perhaps originating with Montaigne's essay "Of Cannibals," contending that primitive man, uncorrupted by civilization, lived the most authentic form of existence.) In his quest for a means of recovering what he imagined to be the ancient powers of the theater, Artaud sought to experience for himself the force of ritual and myth which he, like so many others, was certain existed in traditional societies.

We should not be surprised that Artaud used this knowledge to create a new form of theater as a vehicle for contemporary myth and ritual. If the work of the shaman was efficacious once, why not again in our time? Like our primitive ancestors, we are still primarily concerned with the questions of life and death, of love and hatred, and of good and evil. Was Artaud a crackpot? Maybe not.

Artaud was one of the first members of the surrealist movement. He was attracted to surrealism because he shared its faith in the healing powers of art and, possibly, because he had been treated for his psychological problems, he shared the surrealists' interest in psychology. Freud's discussion of dreamwork unveiled to the surrealists the "mechanisms of inspiration, lyricism and poetic creation" (Rosemont 11). The surrealists felt that the dream could be transformed into a work of art and thereby made visible, a means by which the conscious mind could communicate with the unconscious mind, and they proposed to heal the breech between the inner and outer self through art. They assumed that the artist possesses a certain special *a priori* knowledge, a form of gnosis unavailable from books or professors, which permits the adjustment "to two planes of reality, no longer visualized as contradictory" (Balakian 132). With this knowledge the poet becomes a healer of the divided soul, a shaman capable of leading others to a vision of the inner self.

The surrealists found other mentors in Georg Hegel and Karl Marx. The Hegelian dialectical theory (thesis, antithesis, synthesis) could also be used to describe their artistic objectives: the meeting of reality with dream to produce a new synthesis, a surreality. Most of the surrealists joined the Communist Party as a sign of their commitment to the struggle against the *status quo*.

Many of the surrealists were veterans of the dadaist movement founded in 1916, in the midst of the First World War, as an expression of revulsion against the war and the civilization which permitted it. The primary objective of the dadaists was to overthrow the existing order, to destroy every cultural artifact produced by bourgeois, consumerist society. Once everything was reduced to rubble, they intended to start from ground zero, from the "dada" uttered by the infant learning to speak, and to re-create society and art.

German dadaists who turned to political activism were put down by the British occupation forces. The French dadaists restricted themselves to often amusing, often shocking, and always inventive forms of cultural activism. The failure to bring down the establishment by means of humor and art alone eventually led them to reject the tactics of dadaism as infantile and ineffective. They in turn associated themselves with the Communist Party, as Franklin Rosemont explains, because it possessed "iron Bolshevik discipline, revolutionary ruthlessness," qualities which they believed could eventually bring down the bourgeois order (39).

Artaud, however, parted ways with them, not because he no longer believed in their artistic concepts, but because he found surrealism incompatible with communism. He continued to see himself as a surrealist, the only true one, even after his break with the movement. Following a solitary path better suited to his unique, tortured personality, Artaud turned his efforts to the creation of a theater of myth and ritual. The theater of myth and its audience, as Artaud saw them, are constantly changing. The form of a myth changes or the myth dies. The audience also changes. A myth which is necessary to it at one time has no meaning at another. Unlike Yeats, who tried to graft together various myths and legends to create his own mythology, Artaud felt it was possible to use extant plays, but presented in a manner which would permit the myth inherent in them to manifest itself.

The first duty of the playwright, Artaud argued, is to do away with the stifling idea of the classics. Each play must be considered in terms of its vitality and not its history or its creator. Artaud's idea of the playwright imposes responsibilities beyond merely writing plays. He must also direct the play. Thus if he undertakes to present a play by Shakespeare or Sophocles he must be prepared to re-create and rescue it from a formalistic tradition which attaches itself to plays like a death mask fixing them "in forms that no longer respond to the needs of the times." If performances of Sophocles' *Oedipus the King* fail to move the masses it is not the fault of the play, but the way in which it is performed. It is not the story of Oedipus with which we should concern ourselves, but the universal ideas embedded in it: "the theme of Incest and the idea that all nature mocks at morality; and there exist somewhere errant forces against which we would do well to guard" (IV, 90).

As in Yeats's experience, contact with Oriental drama in 1931, the Balinese Theater in this case, gave Artaud a concrete example of what had been, up to now, partially experimented with or left in the realm of theory. The Balinese theater was made up of real people and solid props, but Artaud experienced it as though it were a divine revelation. Artaud witnessed, as he says, the "*the revelatory side of matter*" which brings the spectator face to face with the mysteries of existence by endowing them with "the metaphysical identity of the concrete and of the abstract." The Balinese Theater, for Artaud, was the theater of the mind come to life. It was "A physical, and nonverbal, idea, in which the theater is included within the limits of all that can happen on the stage, independently of the written text" (IV, 67, 72, 83).

Artaud was impressed by the totality of effect: the unity of music, gesture, color, costume and myth: "What is marvelous is that a sensation of richness, of fantasy, of generous prodigality is given off from the spectacle controlled by a bewildering minutiae of details and consciousness" (IV, 67). The importance of the physical spectacle convinced Artaud that it is not enough to be a playwright. The new form of theater needs a new kind of creator: "a sort of magical director, a master of sacred ceremonies" (IV, 72). The *metteur en scène* is more than the interpreter of a literary work. In addition it is his task to breathe life into art by restoring its former primitive religious power: "to return to it its primitive ends, it is to replace it in its religious and metaphysical perspective, to reconcile it with the universe" (IV, 84). Artaud wished to touch the spectator in every possible manner, to involve every sense. The effect he aimed for was an overwhelming sensation of truth. The spectator would be carried away by "a whirlwind of superior forces" (IV, 99).

Characteristic of myth, as Artaud saw it, is its expression of the evil which underlies all human nature. All action, he writes, has its source in evil: "Good is willed, it is the result of an act. Evil is permanent" (IV, 122). Myth is an expression of evil in action and, by extension, of those willed acts of good. The goal of theater should be to bring the evidence of this evil to the attention of the conscious mind. The conscious mind seeks to ignore its innate evil and its self-ignorance makes it all the more susceptible to evil. The only valid subject matter for theater is that which tears away the false mask of civilization and reveals us as we are despite our resistance to the truth. Myth, for Artaud, is reflected in our dreams and in living legends. A legend lives and becomes myth because it is a true expression of the thoughts and feelings of those who turn to it. It presents the spectator with "trustworthy precipitates of dreams, where his taste for crime, his erotic obsessions, his savagery, his day-dreams, his utopian sense of life and things, even his cannibalism overflow, ..." (IV, 109).

In the history of the Cenci family, previously treated in play form by Shelley and in a short narrative by Stendhal, Artaud thought he had found sufficient evil to mirror the contemporary soul. The story of the Cencis is permeated with evil—murder, incest, revenge, avarice, parricide, torture and executions—to Artaud's mind the perfect subject for a modern mystery play. Everything, from the lighting to the movement of the curtains, was to be under his control. "In a spectacle which I direct, I DON'T WANT even a wink of the eye which isn't mine" (V, 262). Artaud said he wanted to make "the spectator participate in the tragedy of the Cencis with his soul and his nerves" (V, 307). Everything was under Artaud's control except the audience. Despite his control of every detail, *Les Cenci* did not live up to the rhetoric of Artaud's stated expectations, and, as a result, is often considered a failure.

It has been said that Artaud had too many detractors intent on seeing him fail, or he was simply too far advanced for his 1935 audience, but this thesis is convincingly set aside by Christopher Innes, who points out that Artaud's audience and the critics were generally sympathetic to his efforts, that Artaud himself was satisfied with the reaction to his stylized presentation (97).

Artaud's contribution to theater grew steadily from the late forties through the sixties, when his influence seemed to be apparent everywhere—in the works of many playwrights including Ionesco, Beckett, Genet, Pinter, in the Living Theater, and elsewhere (Simon 76). Artaud and Yeats helped give the theater a new direction. They sought to give the spectacle a greater importance in relation to the written text. Both worked against the theater of naturalism and enthusiastically for a theater of myth and ritual. They should be judged for their practical contributions as well their visions of a new form of theater.

Artaud is described by Susan Sontag as a modern-day shaman whose spiritual voyage yields "nothing for the reader except intense discomfort of the imagination" (lvii). The intensity of the discomfort is magnified perhaps by the frustration that comes with the realization that neither Artaud nor Yeats, despite all their rummaging about in the storehouse of ancient myths and stories, found a road to salvation or to the creation of a new age. It is difficult to read their essays without hoping that they could have succeeded somehow. Nevertheless they experimented with and contributed to the development of a new kind of esthetic for the theater. They helped inspire the dramatists who are discussed in the following pages. A major difference, however, is that the playwrights who followed largely ignored the myths and legends of the past, in favor of treating the present in such a way that it takes on a mythical aspect which transforms the theater into a place of metaphysical enlightenment.

It may seem strange to include Bertolt Brecht in a discussion of a healing, metaphysical drama; however, though his rhetoric sets him apart, in practice he has much in common with the other dramatists discussed here. Like the others, Brecht rejected realistic drama and the idea of the classics, because he felt they no longer spoke to the basic needs of humanity. He also experimented with ritual forms of drama, often drawing inspiration from virtually the same sources, such as the Japanese Noh theater and Chinese drama, while proclaiming a radically different goal: to drive emotional involvement out of the theater so the spectator could react logically.

Although Brecht intellectually accepted the Nietzschean world view—that God is dead and that man is no more than a transient entity in a changing world—it was, as Ronald Speirs points out, inadequate to satisfy his subjective need for an ordered universe in which human needs came first. Brecht's early plays, which show different aspects of man liberated from all social conventions and values, also reflect his dissatisfaction with the human condition. As Speirs points out, *Baal* represents "Brecht's early sympathy with the transient individual, and his understanding that men may be ruthless in the pursuit of happiness simply because they are 'only here once'" (13).

However much he sympathized with the *carpe diem* philosophy of Baal, Brecht found it difficult to reconcile himself to the suffering, the anarchic self-interest and social disorientation which accompanies it. Kragler, in *Jungle of Cities*, is a product of the same environment that produced Baal, as are the characters of *Mahagonny*, but, instead of flourishing as a result of the new freedom, they suffer. Brecht's subjective reaction compelled him to find a way to reconstitute the comparatively paradisical world that existed before Nietzsche: in other words, he yearned for the unity of values, beliefs and goals that Christianity once gave to the West. Lacking such values, the characters in *Mahagonny*, says Spiers, "collapse into an anarchic state of nature in which each man is irredeemably encapsulated in his individuality" (164).

Mahagonny was the last major work by Brecht before he committed himself to Marxism. In Marxism he found a reason for existence. Not only did it promise to be a means of solving the material needs of humanity, it also provided him, as Spiers says, with a sense of "community, of moral justification and historical mission" (172). The uses to which Brecht put Marxism in his plays will be discussed in the next chapter, but his reasons for using it will be dealt with here.

Simply put, Brecht wanted to orient his audience and show how to change the world we live in. Brecht wanted to teach the terrible truth he had learned from Nietzsche: that humanity is alone in the universe. Then he wanted to add the idea that each person is responsible for making the universe livable. Theater must show "the world as it changes (and also how it may be changed)" (Willett 79). In the characteristically flip Brechtian manner, he wrote, "It is scarcely possible to conceive of the laws of motion if one looks at them from a tennis ball's point of view" (Willett 193). A better perspective is provided by art: "it is precisely theatre, art and literature which have to form the 'ideological superstructure' for a solid, practical rearrangement of our age's way of life" (Willett 23).

There is a Platonic aspect to Brecht's use of art as a source of metaphysical orientation which is illustrated in this quotation from his stories about Mr. Keuner:

> Mr. K. saw an old chair of great beauty of workmanship somewhere and bought it. He said: I hope to get a few ideas as I reflect what kind of life it must be where a chair such as this would not be conspicuous and the pleasure taken in it be neither disgraceful nor make one stand out. (qtd. in Jauss 27)

When he discussed his theories of art, Brecht used the language of sociology; he spoke of being scientific and of ideological thinking, but as the example above demonstrates, he was aiming for a metaphysical enlightenment not unlike that discussed by Artaud or Yeats.

Brecht devised what he called epic theater to raise the individual above the level of the tennis ball, to provide the knowledge necessary for action. The epic theater, he wrote, arouses the spectator's "capacity for action" and "forces him to take decisions" (Willett 37). In the "Short Organum for the Theater," he wrote:

> We need a type of theatre which not only releases the feelings, insights and impulses possible within the particular historical field of human relations in which the action takes place, but employs and encourages those thoughts and feelings which help transform the field itself. (Willett 190)

The objective of the various alienation techniques associated with the epic theater was to make the obvious perceptible: "to free the socially-conditioned phenomena from that stamp of familiarity which protects them from our grasp" (Willett 192).

Epic theater, in order to arrive at the underlying meaning of social situations, "traces out all their inconsistencies." Eschewing realistic imitation for ritual abstraction, Brecht distorted reality through the use of masks, gesture and choreography. The differences between people disappear in a combination of elements sharing common characteristics. This form of realism conforms to a definition Brecht borrowed from Engels: "the 'reproduction of typical people under typical conditions'" (Willett 246). Because Brecht's characters are oppressed, they wear masks survive. Brecht took the social mask, which in most of us is so alized that it seems natural, and made it visible by means of es intended to simplify and universalize the experience of poraries.

Brecht's early years as a playwright, immediately following World War I, were influenced by expressionism, a German relative of dadaism, and later by surrealism. Brecht abandoned expressionism because, although it brought modern man's anguish to the fore, it failed to provide him with guidance; however, as Ronald Gray points out, expressionism also consisted of Nietzschean and Marxist elements that he carried with him into the later stages of his career as a dramatist:

> Expressionist works went on, expressing belief in the 'New Man,' spreading a message of love and brotherhood, and of a more intense Dionysian existence: there was in them an incompatible combination of Marxist ideals for society and Nietzschean ideals for individuals, total integration and total self-realization. (16)

Brecht continued to use expressionist and surrealist techniques, because they coincided with his idea of true realism which he found in the works of Cervantes, Swift, Grimmelshausen, Dickens, Voltaire, and Hasek, none of whom were interested in surface realism, but rather in distorting reality until its underlying truth become inescapably evident (Willett 114). Common to most of them, and to Brecht as well, is a taste for humor, exaggeration and satire. The realism of a work, Brecht argued, cannot be judged by its form, but by its content.

The exact nature of Brecht's means and ends has been the subject of considerable confusion and discussion. Much of the difficulty hinges on the meaning of epic theater and the *Verfremdungeffekt* ("A-effect") by means of which Brecht proposed to create for the working classes an entertaining and enlightening vision of the world.

The A-effect is supposed to limit the audience's emotional involvement with a play so it can rationally reflect about its meaning. "The new alienations are only designed to free socially-conditioned phenomena from that stamp of familiarity which protects them against our grasp today" (Willett 193). Brecht's expectations for the A-effect were, at first, extremely high, and, as his essays show, diminished as experience taught him its limitations. At first, he seemed to believe he could ban all forms of emotion from the theater. Later, he limited himself to trying to exclude empathy alone. In the end, only the critics, who took Brecht's essays literally, remained to insist that emotion be banned (Fuegi, *Essential* 175; Fuegi, *Chaos* 32).[3]

The content of the play was to be transmitted by means of a variety of theatrical effects which Brecht arranged under the rubric of epic theater. Many of these elements were intended to bring about the A-effect. However, instead of inhibiting emotion, they encouraged it, for the simple reason that, regardless of their intended purpose, these techniques are ritualistic and, inescapably, engage the spectator on the emotional level.

In part, Brecht's use of ritual effects was intended to make characters more abstract and universal, and to prevent the audience from associating the actor with the character being performed. After the fashion of the Noh theater, Brecht had the actors refer to the character being performed in the third person, or reading their lines instead of reciting them from memory. Having the action stop while the characters sing a song about their condition, or while they move the stage props around, is also intended to draw attention to the ensemble rather than individual actors. A dramatic scene with traditional acting might be

---

[3] Unlike many students of Brecht who studied his work from the point of view of his theories, John Fuegi has given priority to Brecht's actual practice in the theater which he frequently finds to be at variance with the playwright's stated intentions. He points out that Brecht, after a decade of trying to make spectators not empathize with Galileo, finally gave in to the inevitable. The following example, given by Fuegi in *The Essential Brecht*, demonstrates the confusion caused when Brecht's public insisted on taking his words literally. In 1956, Brecht began the production of *Galileo* which the Berliner Ensemble presented in Paris. Critics accused the Ensemble "of having 'dramatized' what was supposed to be an 'epic' play and of having given it a 'tragic focus.'" The critics misplaced their ire, says Fuegi, because they did not know that Brecht himself was responsible, otherwise "they would not have directed their wrath at the helpless fire brigade, but against the man who set the fire" (175).

succeeded by a lyrical interlude of song or by the interjection of the third person. While Brecht never gave up trying to find ways to make the audience think, he always kept in mind that theater must give pleasure and made sure these ritual effects were esthetically pleasing (*Theatre* 44-45).

Brecht used songs to tie scenes together and to underscore important traits in his characters. Their lyrics are often a poetic expression of the moral of the play as exemplified by the "Song of Solomon." By placing didactic weight on the lyrics of his songs, Brecht again cleverly combined didacticism with pleasure, but he never managed to do away with emotion.

From the beginning of his career as a dramatist, Brecht experimented with ways of impeding empathy and other emotions, but the certitude that the A-effect is possible came from his experience with oriental drama in the person of Mei Lan-Fang. Whereas Yeats, upon seeing Mr. Ito, discerned a form of art which bypassed the intellect directly appealing to the emotions, and Artaud, seeing the Balinese theater, discovered a way to bring myth and ritual to the Western stage, Brecht claimed he had found a way to keep the spectator from identifying with the stage performance.

"The subconscious is not at all responsive to guidance," says Brecht in "Alienation Effects in Chinese Acting," an essay written in 1936 after he had seen Mei Lan-Fang perform in Moscow (*Theatre* 91-99). The Chinese theater seemed to offer a way to short-circuit the natural empathy of the spectator and make his mind "more responsive to guidance." Speaking of the Chinese actor, Brecht writes: "Acceptance or rejection of their actions and utterances was meant to take place on a conscious plane, instead of, as hitherto, in the audience's subconscious." The conscious nature of Chinese acting—in other words, the situations in which the actor clearly shows an awareness of repeating somebody else's action as opposed to the realist stage where actor and audience are involved, as closely as possible, in a *real* experience—supposedly causes the actor and the audience to be observers of an act which they can judge on its various merits without, at the same time, being participants in the emotion shown.

It is also clear from the same essay on Chinese acting that the reaction of the audience to Mei Lang-Fang's performance did not conform to Brecht's desires: "one or two people behaved as if they were present at the death of a real girl. Possibly their attitude would have been all right for a European production, but for a Chinese it was unspeakably ridiculous" (*Theatre* 95). Despite evidence to the contrary, Brecht went on to theorize about the "A-effect" in Chinese acting. He assumed that the effect of Oriental theater on himself and other Europeans, with such a different theater tradition, was equal to or greater on the Chinese. There is no indication that Brecht considered the possibility that the Chinese might not be "alienated" by their art. On the contrary, he was so intent on finding ways to do away with empathy that he saw what he was looking for.

In his essays, Brecht never presented a completely successful dampening of the emotions. For example, in 1929, Helene Wiegel played Jocasta in a deliberate, unemotional manner in order to emphasize Sophocles' words and not Jocasta's emotions. But, Brecht complained, the spectators were "plunged in self-identification with the protagonist's feelings, virtually the whole audience failed to take part in the moral decisions of which the plot is made up."

Brecht never did get the "A-effect" to work properly, and, by the early 1950s, he was, in principle, actually willing to accept emotional responses in his audiences, as he had always been in practice. His experiments proved that the emotions cannot be purged from the theater through ritual effects, that, on the contrary, they provoke various forms of emotional participation. Yeats and Artaud could not rearrange the unconscious minds of their audiences, and Brecht could not force them to think, but they did make playwrights re-consider the nature of drama, its objectives and means.

Although Yeats and Artaud failed to return to the theater its sacred, healing role, they nevertheless transformed modern drama. They restored its tragic vision. They reminded playwrights that the vast estate of the theater contains elements of the sacred, the ability to give concrete expression to our metaphysical thoughts, the ability to create new myth and rituals for our time, the ability to restore value and meaning to an absurd universe.

Chapter Two

Brecht: The Marxist Myth-Maker

Amidst the political and social chaos of the Weimar Republic and the nihilism of the arts, Communism gave Brecht order, a set of priorities, a means of interpreting empirical information about the world and goals to achieve. The need for such a vision is reflected in Brecht's pre-Marxist work. In *Drums in the Night*, for example, Andrew Kragler returns home after four years as a prisoner of war in Africa to find Anna, his fiancée, pregnant and engaged to a man who became wealthy while shirking his military obligation. Despondent, Kragler prepares to commit suicide by joining the ranks of the doomed Spartacist revolutionaries, but Anna, who has followed him in the streets, convinces him that she still loves him and wants him back; whereupon Kragler renounces war and society to go home with Anna. "I'm a louse and the louse is going home." Aside from "lying in bed . . . multiplying myself so as not to perish from the earth," Kragler finds no other reality worth living for. "Cheap theatricals, that's all it is. There's some boards and a paper moon and a butcher shop in back— that's the only real part" (*Jungle* 161).

In a similar vein, the struggle between Slink and Garga in *The Jungle of Cities* leads nowhere. Looking back on this play in 1954, Brecht said: "I wanted my new play to show the conclusion of a 'fight for fighting's sake,' a fight with no objects except to decide who is 'the best man'" (qtd. in ASTA). Except for fighting for the fun of it, Brecht seemed to say there is no other meaning to life or real communication between people:

SCHLINK: And never, George Garga, there will never be an outcome to
this fight— never an understanding?
GARGA: No, there won't.
SHLINK: But you'll get away, with nothing but your life?
GARGA: It's better to have that life than any other. (84)

The change in the quality and depth of Brecht's characters is
apparent from the moment he brings the Marxist perspective to
his work. Likewise, his situations have both purpose and
direction.

Of course Brecht was neither the first nor the last to give
Marx a literary dimension; what makes him stand out from the
others is the path he followed and that, unlike the others, he
successfully combined his didactic ends with those of creating
works that give pleasure to the audience. One reason for his
success was that he selected, perhaps inadvertently, those aspects
of Marx, described as mythical by Robert Tucker, which are best
suited for the theater. In his study of the development of the
thought of Karl Marx, Tucker demonstrates how Marx created a
modern myth in which the main protagonists are personifications
of Labor and Capital, "the monstrously greedy My Lord Capital
and the enslaved and exploited Collective Worker" (239).

Although a Marxist might object that his ideology is sullied
by the association with myth, such a reaction could only be
termed an emotional response to the word itself. Marx, like Freud,
described the alienation of the conscious self from the unconscious
self. His contribution was to attribute the split within the
individual, this self-alienation, to exterior economic causes, that is,
the exploitation of labor by capital. What was hitherto perceived
as an individual problem is thus identified with the class struggle:
the conflict between the individual, acting alone or as a member of
a group, and the forces of oppression.

Regardless of how it is stated, the conflict exists and,
considering the diffuse nature of coercion in modern society, it is
felt by all of its members regardless of their social status or wealth.

The myth, derived from Marxist thought, verifies the existence of the conflict between what the individual is, or wishes to be, and the pressures to suppress one's true self in deference to the demands of society. This is an idea to which Brecht often gave expression when he asserted that the presence of virtue in the citizens of a nation is not a sign of a happy people. Following Marx, Brecht further condensed and abstracted the experiences of the masses into representative situations involving a handful of equally representative characters of whom only two or three could be fully developed.

Today, when the human being has to be seen as the "sum of all social circumstances," the epic form is the only one that can embrace these processes which serve the drama as matter for a comprehensive picture of the world (Willett 46). In the choice of situations, for Brecht it was important not to represent the central or most decisive events of an era; however, it was essential that the events be representative not necessarily of their historical context, but of ours thereby permitting the spectator to comprehend the logic of the social forces shaping the life of each individual.

In order to make evident the conflict between the authentic self and the abstract self, Brecht resorted to a doubling of personality. As a consequence of this doubling, his characters become more abstract and their personal conflicts are transformed into a mythical clash between man and the superhuman forces of society.

A graphic example of the split is found in the personality of the Good Woman of Setzuan whose quixotic nature requires its own Sancho to protect her and make possible her desire to help others. The Shen-Te/Shui-Ta combination is an irreducible Marxist model of the human personality caught in an imperfect world. In Shen-Te Brecht dramatized Marx's idea of the authentic person. Shui-Ta, who, appropriately, comes into existence whenever she puts on his mask, is the abstract personality Shen-

Te creates in order to survive. She-Te is charged by the gods to live according to the rules of heaven, but finds that, in this world, such a course is impossible. As she says in her apology to the gods:

> Your injunction
> To be good and yet to live
> Was a Thunderbolt
> It has torn me in two
> But to be good to others
> And myself at the same time
> I could not do it. (136)

According to Brecht, to preserve one's humanity and to survive requires incompatible qualities. Shen-Te's positive human traits: love, instinctiveness, a sense of human equality and justice, are irreconcilable with Shui-Ta's survivalist traits: the insistence on contractual bonds, whether fair or not, such as those between employer and worker, hierarchical relations between people and the dominance of reason.

In some of Brecht's plays the elements of the split personality, clearly delineated in the double nature of the Good Woman of Setzuan, are either divided between two or more characters or they coexist uneasily in a single personality. The authentic self of Shen-Te is also typical of Joan Dark, Simone Machard, the Young Comrade, Grusha and Old Dogsborough. Shui-Ta's fellow scoundrels include: Pierpoint Mauler, Soupeau and Arturo Ui. In Mother Courage, Galileo and Puntilla these characteristics are mixed as they are in all humans and they assert themselves according to the situations in which the characters are placed. Mother Courage and Galileo are, perhaps, Brecht's greatest characters because they are at once rounded, human characters who also manage to give concrete expression to the violently opposed elements of their dual natures.

In addition to changing his characters, the influence of Marx is also evident. in the choice of situations. Again, here, although he disliked the Czech critic, Brecht practiced what Lukács advised; he selected situations on the periphery of great events. However, contrary to Lukács, with the exception of *Galileo,* Brecht seemed to prefer situations, not because they illuminate "the social and human motives" of a certain historical period, but for the way they are experienced in our own time (Lukács 42).

In The *Visions of Simone Machard,* which is set in June, 1940, in a French town about to be captured by the advancing German army, the heroine, Simone Machard, who represents the resistance of the entire French nation, is only a simple, little country girl. Her employer, Soupeau, represents the hypocritical, moneyed class which welcomes the Germans and eagerly cooperates with them. Mother Courage follows in the train of whichever of the opposing armies fate has placed her. The central concern of the play is not with questions of military strategy, or the personalities of kings and generals, but with the suffering and the struggle of the little people to survive and even turn a profit. In *The Caucasian Chalk Circle,* Grusha is only accidentally on the spot when the Governor is led to his death by the Iron-Shirts. She spends the rest of the war "on the other side of the mountain" doing whatever is necessary to survive and to protect the child until Simon returns. The "love story" of MacHeath and Polly is played out in the London underworld far from the monumental preparations for the Queen's coronation. In each case, Brecht is concerned with showing the circumstances in which the common people are obliged to live and their reactions to them. Brecht did not try to create "real" people; instead he wanted characters whose destiny and psychology are representative of social trends and historical forces (Fuegi, *Essential* 131, 146). "The characters," as Brecht said, "are not simply portraits of living people, but are rearranged and formed in accordance with ideas" (Willett 278)

A brief review of some of Brecht's major plays demonstrates how his use of doubling serves to give concrete expression to Marx's mythical vision of the forces which define modern man. Brecht's recasting of the story of Joan of Arc in the Chicago stockyards presents not a struggle between people, but a mythical revelation of the power of social and economic forces to destroy those who would oppose them and the ability of the same forces to raise their chosen representatives above the ranks of mere mortals.

Mauler, the king of the stockyards, is invested with a superhuman Midas' touch which increases his wealth and power even when he seeks to escape it. Graham, one of his fellow businessmen, can only describe Mauler in terms suitable for a god:

> There's no hindering
> This monster in his climb: nature to him
> is merchandise, even the air's for sale.
> What's in our stomachs he resells to us.
> He gets rent out of caved-in houses, money
> from rotten meat; stone him, he's sure to change
> the stones to money; he's so wild for money
> so natural in this unnaturalness
> that even he cannot deny its power.
> He's soft himself, you know, does not love money
> cannot bear misery, cannot sleep at night. (38)

Mauler, himself, confesses to Joan that he is only the mask, the embodiment, of a force which he does not and cannot control. He tells her that is impossible for him to escape its power:

> it would be as if
> a fly stopped holding back an avalanche.
> I would become a nothing and it would keep on
> going over me. (81)

In remorse for the life he has led, Mauler attempts to find consolation in Christianity, as professed by the Black Straw Hats, the Salvation Army type organization to which Joan belongs. He finds, on being scornfully rejected by Snyder, the head of the mission, that they prefer his money to his soul. The Chorus of Black Straw Hats echoes Snyder, albeit more gently:

> His heart
> he brought to us, but not his money.

Therefore our hearts are moved, but
our faces are long. (106)

In any case, Mauler's effort to find consolation and salvation
does not entail his destruction, because he cannot escape his fate
as ruler of the stockyards any more than Oedipus can avoid
murdering his own father. He returns to his old life without
hesitation when the desperate meat packers and stock breeders
entreat him to make the system function again. In the person of
Mauler an inhuman force acquires a human face. Brecht, having
revealed the authentic self hidden behind it, then replaced the
abstract mask of power on its human victim. At the same time,
however, the force remains inhuman and independent of its
human host.

In describing his own personal insignificance, Mauler also
explains why Joan's struggle will be futile and why she will be
destroyed by the very forces that make him so powerful. At the
same time, he is indirectly explaining why Joan will be unable to
save him and, through him, rescue the workers from their misery.

Joan, on the other hand, is doomed to die from the beginning
because she refuses to yield to the system and, worse yet, because
she attempts to take it on by herself. Brecht advocated a united
resistance by the workers under the leadership of the
Communists, but this, in terms of the struggle between the
individual and society as it is presented on the stage, is little more
than a symbolic alternative. When Joan announces that she
intends to learn the truth about the conditions of the workers, she
is warned by her fellow missionaries to keep above the battle,
which, for Brecht, is a euphemism for siding with the exploiters:

The meddler in a fight becomes its victim! . . .
you will disappear in dirt!
Nothing but dirt is stuffed into the mouths
Of those who ask without caution. (37)

Joan refuses to heed the warnings of her colleagues and begins a ritual movement towards her death in an atmosphere charged with Christian symbolism.

Joan makes three "descents" into the depths of the stockyards. In the beginning she is unaware of the true humanity of their workers and the fact that they are oppressed; she assumes that their abject condition is a result of their personal vices and failures. When she leads her first unsuccessful march of the Black Hat shock troop in search of lost souls, she naively explains to the workers that their situation is a result of their lack of interest in higher things and laziness. Her second descent is at the side of Sullivan Slift, Mauler's lieutenant, who seeks to prove to her the wickedness of the poor. This time, however, Joan learns from what she sees instead of imposing her own interpretation upon it. She finally realizes that morality is too dear for the pockets of the poor:

Not the wickedness of the poor
Have you shown me, but
The poverty of the poor . (51)

When Joan attempts to act on her newfound knowledge, she begins to learn the truth about the forces which control the world.

Despite Mauler's apparently genuine affection for her (he seems to see in Joan an aspect of himself which has been suppressed as a result of his complete submission to the forces of the marketplace) and his promises to help change things, nothing happens. The system, as described in this Brechtian vision of Hell, feeds on the misery of the poor and Mauler would be acting against his nature if he effected real change. When Joan recognizes that she cannot rely on Mauler and his cohorts, she expels them, as Christ did the money changers, from the house of God. The reward for her behavior is expulsion from the ranks of the Black Straw Hats. As Snyder explains to the business community, their interests complement each other: The mission cannot survive without the financial support of the rich, and the businessmen need the Black Straw Hats in order to distract the attention of the workers from the true causes of their misery and to direct it heavenward.

In the end, Joan decides to act alone. Her final descent into the stockyards follows and it lasts three days. She is tempted by the possibility of practical action in the form of giving her services to the Communist strike organizers. Joan agrees to deliver a message to the workers calling on them to hold out just a little longer. The success of the strike now depends on Joan, but, once she is in the stockyards again, she chooses not to deliver the message and to carry on the struggle alone. In behavior resembling that of the Young Comrade in *The Measures Taken*, she disobeys orders because she permits her humanity to intrude on her duty; she sets back the organizing efforts of the workers and, as a consequence of her failure, dies. In a vision, Joan recognizes the folly of her ways, but it is too late. She has been broken and is dying.

Joan's heroic behavior does not go unnoticed; she is received at the mission by the Black Straw Hats, the slaughterers, the stock breeders and the wholesalers as a heroine. As she is dying of pneumonia, she makes a speech which is at once a denunciation of Mauler, a denial of God and a revelation of the split nature of the world:

> You see, there's a gulf between top and bottom, bigger
> Than between Mount Himalaya and the sea.(120)

However, her words are drowned out by the "Hosannas" of the meat packers.

The dead Joan is transformed into a symbol of the very forces she sought to combat. As Slift says: "We will set her up as a saint and deny her no respect. On the contrary, her revelation here will serve as proof that we hold humaneness in high regard" (118). The system is so voracious and all-consuming that it can turn a profit even on the remains of its victims; just as it does in the case of the hapless Luckerniddle, who slips and falls into a boiler to emerge from the slaughterhouse as bacon. In a similar manner, Joan's spiritual legacy falls, by default, into the hands of her enemies.

The significance of Brecht's combination of ideology with theater becomes clearer if we consider two plays which are related to *Saint Joan of the Stockyards* by content and the fact that all three plays were written about the same time, between 1928 and 1930. *Happy End* precedes the other two plays and itself is a light-hearted re-casting of *The Threepenny Opera* whose success it was intended to exploit. Set in Chicago, *Happy End* pits the Salvation Army against local gangsters in a comic conflict which reappears later in *Saint Joan of the Stockyards* in a more tragic mode. The other play, *The Measures Taken*, is a purely ideological *lehrstücke*, a didactic play, in which the issues underlying Joan Dark's struggles and death—and, indeed, all of Brecht's subsequent plays—are treated in a straightforward manner. This play and *The Yea-Sayers* and the *Nay-Sayers*, which were adaptations of the Japanese Noh play *Taniko*, brought the influence of oriental drama into Brecht's work in 1929, about the same time he turned to Marx for a sociological perspective. According to Andrzej Wirth, the two influences were complementary:

> Buddhism, however, with its worship of Bodhisattvas . . . [and] its stress on *satori* (enlightenment), provides a closer analogy to Marxism than Christianity . . . .
> For Brecht, the noh's mystic initiation seemed translatable into ideological indoctrination, its concept of *yugen* (the search for what lies beneath the surface) into a vision of the scientific era, Zen's non-verbal, contemplative introspection as the way to truth into a non-verbal activist attitude, the Noh's spirit of a mystic sect searching for salvation by means of charms and spells into party discipline. And finally, Brecht shared an affinity with the dialectical reasoning of the Noh drama. (602)

From Wirth's point of view, Brecht secularized the Japanese model; however, seen from the perspective of this discussion of his work, it can be said that the Noh drama provided Brecht with yet another means of bringing out and further emphasizing the mythical, metaphysical aspects of Marxism.

The Measures Taken was intended to illustrate the need for the individual to submit to Party discipline as a means of assuring the success of their common revolutionary goals. According to Brecht, the Young Comrade is a revolutionary as far as his feelings are concerned, but he possesses too little discipline and fails to follow his reason, so that he unwittingly becomes a serious danger to the movement (Wulbern 100). The questions of discipline are considered by a Control Chorus before which the Three Agitators, who accompanied the Young Comrade on a mission to China, explain why they executed him. The Young Comrade's failure lies in his inability to suppress his natural self. Before leaving for China, the agitators are reminded by the Leader: "One and all of you are nameless and motherless, blank pages on which the revolution writes its instructions." In a ritual donning of Chinese masks, the revolutionaries hide their Russian and German origins to become "fighters, Chinese, born of Chinese mothers, with yellow skin, speaking Chinese in fever and sleep" (82). The need to wear masks is proof that the world is too dangerous for individuals to reveal their authentic selves. In order to fight the abstract forces which oppress them, they are obliged to willingly lend themselves, their lives and their strength, to be subsumed by yet another abstract force created to lead the fight for liberation.

Unfortunately for the mission, the Young Comrade cannot prevent his personal feelings from intruding upon his mission. As a result, he subverts his own efforts and those of his comrades by acting impetuously to find an immediate solution to the human problems which confront him. He finds a way to ease the burden of coolies pulling barges. He intervenes in the arrest of a worker distributing revolutionary leaflets. Out of disgust, he refuses to negotiate with a capitalist arms dealer. In each case the cause of revolution is set back. The coolies whose suffering has been mitigated will be less willing to revolt. The organizing activities of the agitators at the factories are curtailed because their cover is exposed. The lack of weapons reduces the revolutionary potential of the masses. In the end, the Young Comrade totally renounces Party discipline and appears to the people of the city, "his naked face, human, open, guileless" (102), to lead them to a premature and abortive revolt. Acting on his own, and without a full knowledge of the situation, the Young Comrade sets back the cause of revolution. In a similar manner, Joan Dark, by not delivering the message for the workers to hold out a little longer, thwarts the possibility of a successful confrontation with Mauler and his associates.

The Young Comrade and Joan are caught in a struggle between superhuman forces whose cruel logic makes no allowance for human weakness; their honesty only betrays them to their enemies. Later, in *Galileo*, Cardinal Barberini will scoff at the idea that the scientist poses some sort of threat to the establishment: "Let us replace our masks, Bellarmin. Poor Galilei hasn't got one" (80). It is no surprise, therefore, that in 1941, when Brecht uses the story of Joan of Arc again in *The Visions of Simone Machard*, his heroine, Simone, is a child of only eleven years.

In one of her dreams, the Angel, who resembles her brother, charges Simone to follow in the footsteps of Joan of Arc and rally the French in their struggle against the Germans. Acting alone, without guile or a sense of the need for covert behavior, Simone exposes herself to the machinations of those who, at least outwardly, have chosen to cooperate with the puppet government led by Colonel Fetain. Brecht linked events in Simone's village to analogous ones in French history, by having the actors playing villagers double as noble characters in the visions where Simone plays the Maid of Orléans. The lesson implicit in this play is that individual effort is doomed unless it is allied to and guided by a force capable of measuring up to the forces of oppression.

In *The Measures Taken* Brecht made the above point too explicit and incurred the wrath of his fellow Communists (163-165). Like the Young Comrade, Brecht committed the error of removing the mask of Party rhetoric and exposing its workings to outside scrutiny (and, inadvertently, suggesting that the authentic person is as unwelcome among Communists as anywhere else). Most of Brecht's plays do not make their political lesson as explicit as in *The Measures Taken* and the other didactic plays; in theory, Brecht wanted the audience to draw its own conclusions from the examples given and not from precept. Mother Courage, Galileo, Shen-Te/Shui-Ta, Puntilla, all of Brecht's characters who manage to survive in this world do so because they have learned to balance their emotional natures against the demands placed on their intellects to survive. Those who cannot adjust to reality are doomed.

With the exception of a few overtly political comments, the love story of *Happy End*, hastily put together by Brecht and Weill, in collaboration with Elizabeth Hauptmann, to cash in on the success of *The Threepenny Opera* (Esslin *Brecht* 298), is basically an apolitical pretext for tying together a collection of songs in the manner of a Broadway musical. Because it is conventional, *Happy End* provides us with a measure of the originality and uniqueness of Brecht's other plays. In the non-ideological context of *Happy End*, the protagonists meet, fall in love, survive all the intrigues against them and marry in the end. Lieutenant Lillian Holiday, an officer in the Salvation Army, bears a surface resemblance to Joan Dark. And, of course, since Brecht saw little difference between gangsters and businessmen, it is not surprising that Bill Cracker, the Chicago gangster, has much in common with Pierpoint Mauler. The two men derive power from their ill-gotten gains. In addition, both men have a sentimental side which makes them susceptible to a missionary's appeal for reform, especially if she is also an attractive woman.

The characters and situations in *St. Joan of the Stockyards*, *Happy End*, *The Threepenny Opera*, and *The Visions of Simone Machard* are closely related. In order to present his audience with a tragic vision of man's feeble struggle to overcome the powers of oppression, Brecht infused his material with his interpretation of Marx. The similarities between *Happy End* and *St. Joan of the*

Stockyards are not profound, for, while Hallelujah Lil and Cracker are mere human beings susceptible to being influenced by one another, Mauler and Holliday cannot change, because they are not mere individuals, but embodiments of forces greater than themselves. Lil bends her Christian principles enough to get drunk with Cracker and to arouse his interest in her as a woman. Likewise, Cracker is willing to skip an important bank robbery in order to be with Lil. Neither character has a destiny which can prevent them from fulfilling their instinctive needs and desires. Holliday and Mauler, on the other hand, do not compromise, they clash, and in their persons the instinctive aspirations of humanity clash with the forces of social and economic reality. It is this metaphysical dimension which sets *Saint Joan of the Stockyards* and *The Measures Taken* apart from *Happy End*.

In Brecht's plays one finds the gap between the ideal and the real expressed in many ways and often on several levels at the same time. Usually the ideal is played against the real in order to emphasize the discrepancy between them and to make the need for change unavoidably obvious. With rare exceptions, such as setting *The Caucasian Chalk Circle* in a Soviet Republic, Brecht also sticks to the real world. A potentially better world appears momentarily in *The Caucasian Chalk Circle* when Azdak, displaying the wisdom of Solomon and the cunning of Odysseus, recognizes a higher form of motherhood and gives Grusha Michael, the child abandoned by the Governor's Wife. Azdak's short rule as judge serves as a visible standard of comparison between the world we live in and the world as it might be. In a similar manner, Puntila's drunken lapses from the ranks of the exploiters reveals a generous and sympathetic being who will never realize his human potential in this world.

In my discussion of *The Caucasian Chalk Circle* I shall show how Brecht utilized his epic techniques to create ritual. In *Galileo* I shall consider the problems involved in creating mythical characters. The techniques used by Brecht to create the A-effect in

The Caucasian Chalk Circle, because they are more distinct than in other plays, lend themselves more readily to analysis. First, Brecht uses the device of a play-within-a-play which constantly reminds the audience it is in the theater. At the same time, this technique makes the dramatic moments more intense and concentrated.

The play itself takes place after World War II among the ruins of a Caucasian village and is a celebration of the just settlement of conflicting claims advanced by two Kolkhoz villages for the same land. The Singer, Arkadi Tscheidse, is invited to entertain with his ballads. While he sings, the story he is recounting comes to life beside him on the stage. With a technique adapted from the Japanese Noh, Brecht set a permanent reminder on the stage to keep the audience from forgetting that it is watching a play. In addition, the Singer serves to speed up the movement of the play and makes sure that the dramatic scenes concentrate only on the heart of each situation. The third scene, for example, begins with Grusha's flight into the mountains with the child and ends with its being taken from her by the Iron-Shirts. The third scene comprises less than one sixth of the play, but is tightly packed with dramatic situations. Grusha is obliged to leave her brother's home because of her sister-in-law's "moral" objections to having an unwed mother around. Grusha buys shelter at the price of marrying a dying peasant who "miraculously" becomes well during the combination wake/wedding celebration and proceeds to make the life of his bride miserable. And just before the return of Simon, Grusha's betrothed, and the coming of the Iron-Shirts, there is another play-within-a-play: Michael, the son of the governor, demonstrates the role of the milieu in determining personality. Michael's little companions reenact the execution of his father, the Governor, and, although he is offered the role of his father, Michael insists upon and gets to play the role of the Governor's executioner.

In the next scene, Azdak stages another play-within-a-play when he sets up a moot court to demonstrate the kind of justice he would dispense if he were judge. In his 1954 production of the play, Brecht used the same actor to play both the Singer and Azdak. By having the same actor perform different roles on different levels of the play, Brecht emphasized the fact that, as in the moot court scene, the spectator is observing a theatrical performance. At the same time the unity and the intensity of the presentation are increased because the attention of the audience, as well as its sympathy, are focused on the actor who combined the personalities of the Singer and Azdak.

The mythical and ritual qualities of the play are reinforced in other ways by the Singer. By introducing the characters and explaining their actions, the Singer does away with the need for a plot. There is also no need for character development of the sort which involves the audience in petty details of the protagonist's life. One can concentrate on the actions themselves. As a result, it is the form of the play, not its content, which determines the nature of the audience's participation. Of course, the use of music and the Singer are only two of the elements used by Brecht which contribute to the ritual effect.

Fuegi's discussion of Brecht's model book for the 1954 staging of *The Caucasian Chalk Circle* and his interviews with some of the participants in that production reveal ritual possibilities not suggested by a reading of the play. Fuegi emphasizes its ritual movement, its unity and powerful emotional effect. He notes that Brecht drew an obvious parallel between Azdak and Christ. The soldiers raise Azdak to the rank of judge by crowning him and placing a robe about his shoulders as the Romans do to Christ when they crown him king of the Jews. Azdak helps the poor where he can. He is later taken off to be hanged as Christ was crucified. In addition, Grusha's flight into the mountains recalls the flight to Egypt. And she is, in effect, the virgin mother of Michael (Fuegi, *Essential* 143-159). In his production, Brecht transferred to the secular stage ritual elements of the passion play whose emotional significance for the spectator precedes their Christian interpretation. Two thousand years of Christian imagery, ingrained in the sensibility of the spectator, could only serve to augment the emotional response to the play.

Fuegi uses the word ritual in a way which is quite common, but which also tends to confuse ritual with myth. Ritual is seen here as the product of countless repetitions of the same act until its superficial, realistic elements are sloughed off and replaced by the abstract elements common to all of them—the universal displacing the historical, as Aristotle might have described it. The elements of this "ritual" are familiar; they include the betrayal of the hero, the hero's trial and execution/punishment, and finally the enlightenment of those whom the hero befriended.

"Once when asked . . . to name the strongest literary influence in his life, Brecht replied . . . 'You will laugh: The Bible!'" (qtd. in Esslin *Brecht* 112). Brecht often played the ideals of Christianity against its actual practice. Moreover, despite his ideological position, his Christian heroes are often his most esteemed. Brecht had nothing against Christians like Joan Dark and Lillian Holiday, except their inability to change the world. His opinion of religion in general is reflected in his ironic use of gods and angels and is emphasized by his demonstration that, while they may be well-intentioned, they are ineffectual. Simone Machard's angel leads her to behave patriotically but does not intervene when the poor child could use some divine help. Likewise, once the gods put Shen-Te on the spot, they are unable to provide a solution for her dilemma.

As playwrights, from the Renaissance on, realized, belief in the Christian God makes tragedy impossible, for it cannot exist where a beneficent, forgiving god awaits the protagonist after the tragic sparagmos. Nietzsche set the deity aside, making tragedy possible once again, and Brecht's *Mother Courage* brings us to the edge of the abyss with an intensity possessed by few twentieth-century plays.

Most of Brecht's protagonists are aware of our human vulnerability in a hostile universe and their first defense is cynicism and an attempt to avoid the values and virtues associated with humanity. When the Commander praises Eilif for his bravery, Mother Courage retorts that the need for virtues like bravery are proof that things are being badly run: "In a good country virtues wouldn't be necessary. Everybody could be quite ordinary, middling, and, for all I care, cowards" (39). Later, in "The Song of the Great Capitulation," she points out that the virtues of the great men in history have served to bring them low:

> God's Ten Commandments we have kept
> And acted as we should
> It has not done us any good. (100)

Nevertheless, as we see in *Mother Courage* and the other plays, a great many virtues are needed merely to survive. Hiding them in a show of cowardice, or even denying them with a pretense of hard-heartedness, may be necessary to live for another day, but it does not define the character.

Mother Courage is virtually all mask, all business, and Brecht intended her to be this way because through her he wanted us to condemn war and those who profit from it. Mother Courage is the epitome of money-grubbing. She gets her name from driving her "cart through the bombardment of Riga like a madwoman, with fifty loaves of bread in my cart. They were going moldy, what else could I do?" (25). She loses her children one by one, because business comes first. Eilif is enlisted by the Recruiting Officer while she dickers with the Sergeant over the price of a belt (32-33). Swiss Cheese is executed while she is trying to raise the money for the bribe to save him, because she refuses to bring her price down (63). Kattrin sacrifices herself to save the city while her mother is away trying to unload unwanted merchandise (110). Mother Courage has few redeeming traits. Bentley cites one scene, excised by Brecht, in which Mother Courage, going against her better judgment, rips up valuable shirts so they can be used as bandages (118). We are supposed to find her unsympathetic because she could have chosen to live otherwise, but in the bleak setting of the play there seems to be little choice. When the Cook invites her to join him in running the little inn in Utrecht, provided she deserts the ugly, unmarriageable Kattrin, Mother Courage refuses (100-101). Brecht's genius for portrayal undermines his didactic goals: we cannot turn against Mother Courage because we have all shared in the defeats and reversals inevitable in our mortal beings. Soviet Critic Boris Sachawa sums up what many audiences have felt at the end of the play:

> The heart of the viewer is unwillingly seized when he sees how hopelessly the wagon has aged, how run down it is, and into what a frightful ruin a formerly energetic, active, and level-headed woman has been changed, who, in spite of her condition, still does not understand its cause: the scene is a terrifying symbol of the tragic fate of an entire people. (qtd. in Fuegi, *Chaos* 125)

Brecht composed *Galileo* during World War II, but continued to revise it until his death. The bombing of Hiroshima convinced him to alter his original thesis that it is each person's duty to aid the progress of science by adding a moral *caveat*. While Galileo is the product of entirely contemporary considerations, Brecht increased its scope and power by setting it in the seventeenth century where his manipulation of historic events creates a correspondence between historical events four hundred years apart. The historical events in the life of Galileo were important only in that, as Brecht said, they serve to illustrate "man's failure to understand the laws governing his life in society" (Willett 133). In selecting the illustrious historical figure, Brecht clearly violated the criteria for the selection of historical characters to which he usually adhered. As a consequence, the historical image of Galileo with its traditional associations created many intractable problems for Brecht, who needed a scientist who could typify qualities not associated with Galileo's historical image. Whatever Brecht might have intended to illustrate, he had to contend with already established attitudes. Joseph Campbell describes Galileo as being of an age when the "hero deed" could still be performed: "When then there was darkness, now there is light; but also, where light was, there now is darkness" (388). American and European schoolchildren who have read about Galileo see him as a giant of his time, a heroic individual who almost single-handedly, and in spite of the mightiest efforts of the Inquisition, changed our relationship with the universe. Brecht, in attempting to remake Galileo into a villain, went against a deeply rooted emotional sympathy for the scientist and found it impossible to overcome.

The difficulties experienced by Brecht in his attempts to regulate audience reaction can be best explained by saying that his work is better suited for arousing emotions than for stimulating intellection. Brecht usually had several political points to make, and to ensure that the spectator remained sufficiently "reasonable," he packed his plays with epic elements. However, he was too good a dramatist to be satisfied with mere propaganda; he did everything necessary, including, as Fuegi repeatedly reminds us, going against his own prescriptions.

Galileo illustrates the gap between Brecht's didactic intent and the actual reaction aroused by his dramatic creation. Despite his achievements, Galileo is not to be admired if Brecht can help it. Brecht emphasizes the unsavory character of his protagonist: Galileo tries to bilk the Venetian senate by posing as the inventor of the telescope discovered in Holland; he peddles his ideas for commercial and military uses without moral qualms; he recants his theory of the solar system and, in effect, temporarily inhibits the movement of scientific progress. "If only he had understood his historical situation dialectically," we are supposed to tell ourselves, "things might have been different." Lack of insight into one's situation, as Sartre has written, explaining the need for a dialectical perspective, keeps one from choosing the proper course of action. "He misunderstood himself at the same moment that he created that which transformed his condition" (28).

Galileo, with the future of humanity in his hands, gives in before the threat of torture because of a softness symbolized by his gourmandise. He lacks the proper attitude of the Young Comrade who sacrifices himself for the good of the Party and, by extension, all humanity. Unfortunately for Brecht, many of Galileo's weaknesses humanize him and make him more attractive to the audience. While his dialectical ability may be defective, the scientist knows a good wine and enjoys his goose liver fried with an apple. His flesh would find the tortures of the Holy Inquisition unbearable. Unlike Prometheus, whom he resembles in many ways, Galileo is not capable of resisting the threat of torture. His love of learning and of good food spring as naturally from him as they do from Brecht's pre-Marxist character, Baal. Galileo explains to Sagredo that he had to trick the Venetian Senate, because he needed money to pay his taxes and to set aside a dowry for his daughter: "And I like to buy books—all kinds of books. Why not? And what about my appetite? I don't think well unless I eat well. Can I help it if I get my best ideas over a good meal and a bottle of wine?" (61).

As he puts on the vestments of the Pope, Barberini reiterates Galileo's statement, only more emphatically: "He has more enjoyment in him than any man I ever saw. He loves eating and drinking and thinking. To excess. He indulges in thinking-bouts! He cannot say no to an old wine or a new thought" (109).

Galileo, like Baal and Azdak (and perhaps Brecht himself), resembles Marx's authentic man in his love of learning, good food and women, and, even though Barberini assumes he is defenseless, without a mask, in the end Galileo saves himself by means of his cunning. When, on Barberini's instructions, he is shown the instruments of torture, he capitulates and, superficially, at least, retains the joys of the flesh at the expense of science. On seeing Galileo yield, the spectator is supposed to compare him to a model such as Azdak, who "is able to make use of the potentialities of his situation, of the chances offered by 'chaos'" (Metscher 141). All of his very human failings are supposed to make Galileo difficult to identify with and, hence, subject to having his actions judged objectively by the spectator. Paradoxically, it is Barberini who is defenseless, for, as he dons the vestments of Pope Urban VIII, he is forced to surrender his defense of science and the truth to satisfy the exigencies of the role he has assumed. As the stage directions tell us at the end of the scene: "*The eyes of* BARBERINI *look helplessly at the* CARDINAL INQUISITOR *from under the completely assembled panoply of* POPE URBAN VIII" (110). As in the plays of Genet, authority and the power to oppress others is not a form of freedom, but is merely another form of submission to the oppressive forces of the world, another form of death in life. The trick, as Galileo and Azdak show us, is to yield as little as possible while retaining as much freedom as possible. Since most of us find ourselves in similar situations, it is easy to empathize with these characters despite Brecht's wishes to the contrary.

Because audiences missed Brecht's point, he revised the play to make Galileo denounce himself in front of the audience:

> for years I was as strong as the authorities, and I surrounded my knowledge to the powers that be, to use it, no, not *use* it, *abuse* it, as it suits their ends. I have betrayed my profession. Any man who does what I have done must not be tolerated in the ranks of science. (124)

Yet, after recanting a second time, this time before the Holy Inquisition of the historical dialectic, one can imagine Galileo muttering: "Yet, I am tolerated . . . even admired."

Galileo is admirable not only in spite of his faults, but also because of them. Regardless of the fact that some one else might eventually come to the conclusions found in the *Discorsi*, Galileo remains their discoverer. Are we supposed to overlook the fact that in Brecht's own play Galileo ruins his eyes because, despite his promises to give up science, he works at night to avoid discovery? The magnitude of his discovery puts him among the ranks of those who bring fire to humanity. He rearranges the movement of our solar system, or rather our concept of it, sending shudders through the ranks of heaven's earthly representatives and inviting their wrath upon himself. Yet Galileo is only human; he cannot endure torture and has only one irreplaceable life.

Galileo wears a Janus mask of good and evil. If he is Promethean in his bringing of new knowledge to the world, if his discoveries mark a watershed in history, the movement from a theologically dominated to a rational scientific universe, he is also responsible for helping pry open a Pandora's box of evils. If his discoveries mean ships can navigate better and more safely on the high seas, they also portend space travel. If his stolen inventions give the Venetian fleet an advantage over its enemies, they are only a part of a series of weapons leading to our unenviable present capacity for self-annihilation.

The telescope fraud, which depends for its success on the covetousness of Venetian commercial and military interests, is similar to Prometheus' tricking Zeus into preferring bones and fat as his proper offering from the human race, rather than the flesh of the bull. This trickster aspect of Galileo, instead of making him unlikable, makes his character more interesting and links him with another mythic figure.

Galileo's personality turns Brecht's tragedy into a comedy in which both evil and good coexist. A heroic pose would have demanded a tragic turn and a more limited, intense protagonist to bring the crisis to a head. Galileo does exactly as he should because he represents a force that cannot be killed or permanently stilled. His response to events simply defuses their tragic implications and asserts, despite the claims of history, that the highest human values are in serving life.

Ionesco erred in his criticism of Brecht: "His man is incomplete and often is only a puppet." Or, when he said, "The Brechtian man is infirm, because his author refuses him his innermost reality" (*Notes* 194). On the contrary, Brecht succeeded because he did not attempt to put "realistic" people on the stage, but because the abstract humanity of his characters often resembles the inner reality of the spectator. Indeed, in the occasional grotesqueness caused by Brecht's striving for the A-effect, the humanity of his characters is magnified to the point where it touches our own. In the same manner we are not repelled by the extravagant gestures of puppets which emphasize what is latent in the real people they imitate.

Aside from his dialectical interpretation of history, Brecht's characters and the situations in which they are obliged to act render to us some of the social and psychological verities of our time. In a world which interprets human behavior in a determinist, or behaviorist, manner, the individual is little more than a complex marionette whose strings are pulled by forces beyond its control, regardless of whether or not these forces are psychological or social and economic. The sometimes pitiful, sometimes magnificent, characters Brecht created fit perfectly well with our own diminished perception of ourselves. Brecht could add lines making Galileo reproach himself for cowardice and cupidity, but we can only sympathize with the characters who bend. Thus, instead of serving Brecht's purposes, his characters affirm their own humanity and escape all attempts to diminish them. This is true of Mother Courage, MacHeath, Puntilla, and even Mr. Peachum. The clash between the human desires and aspirations of his characters as they contend with the forces of economic and political necessity culminate in tragic moments of metaphysical illumination.

Chapter Three

Self and Other in the Plays of Jean Genet

If we are to understand Genet's plays, it is necessary above all to understand his analysis of self and other and how he uses the theater to give substance to his healing vision. The most direct route to the mystery in Genet's work is the well known story of his decision to become a thief, to accept a social role unjustly attributed to him, because his adoptive parents and the society of which they were a part refused to recognize the innocent child he was. It is important to focus on the struggle between self and other, because this is where he speaks most intimately and revealingly about himself and his audience, about the social mask which suffocates the authentic self. Inspired by the example of Artaud, Genet recast essential patterns of human behavior into myths for the theater. In Genet we have struggles between master and servant, black and white, colonizer and colonized, but the underlying patterns are always combinations of the same motifs: self versus other, sham and illusion against the authentic being behind the mask. Whatever the role attributed to Genet by society, he was an artist and through art he redeemed himself; now, by means of this same art, he offered the world a healing vision of reality.

For Genet, the theater is a distorting mirror wherein the soul of the spectator is captured and reflected:

> I go to the theater in order to see myself, on the stage (reconstituted into a single character or with the help of a single character multiple and in the form of a story) as I would know, or wouldn't dare see or dream

myself, and as I know myself to be. The actors have means that permit
them to show me to myself, and to show me naked, in solitude and joy.
(10-11)

Through the interplay of realism and sham, the mundane and the
bizarre, Genet conjured up a metaphysical vision of the
contemporary world. Those who dwell on the surface strangeness
of his plays see merely the expression of the private myth of a
poète maudit [an "apostle of treachery," in the words of Edmund
White (555)]—but Genet's vision has much broader relevance. The
"real" underworld, had he intended to show it, could have been
presented in a realistic manner. Instead we are given "that state of
metaphysical strangeness" (*Théâtre* 96), Roland Barthes deemed
essential to make the underlying reality of the everyday world
evident.

The individual shapes society and, in turn, is shaped by it.
However, society being larger and more powerful than any of its
members, is able to manipulate the individual mercilessly. Many
of Genet's characters seek consolation for their frustration and
suffering by attempting to trade the social role which oppresses
them for another. This endeavor is fruitless because it merely
results in the exchange of one kind of oppression for another: the
old mask is replaced by a new one. Most of Genet's characters fail
to free themselves from the power of the mask, some are caught in
midstream while attempting to make the changeover and are
destroyed. Others succeed temporarily only to be entangled in yet
another sterile, narcissistic fantasy. The possibility of an authentic
existence is glimpsed occasionally and then lost again among the
countless illusions which seduce the individual into trading one
mask for another.

Genet deconstructed modern myths comparable to what
anthropologists variously call charter, legitimation, or explanatory
myths. That is, myths which, among other things, justify "socio-
structural discrepancies in contemporary life" (Yamba 110), or
"sanction particular attitudes and behavior" (Haviland 389). In

some cases these myths serve to explain and rationalize the domination of one group of people by another.

When asked by an interviewer to explain his support for the Palestinians, Genet distinguished between the "real" world and the "grammatical" world (1987, 72). The ability of the grammatical world, in the guise of Orientalist literary myths about Arabs, "almost" out of *The Thousand and One Nights*,[4] to determine his perceptions was dispelled only after he met Palestinian *fedayeen* on a visit to Jordan in 1970. He found, as he said, "a people whose every gesture had a density, a real weight" (1987, 70).

In his plays Genet sought to cast out similar myths by showing how they supported social, political and racial structures leading to the oppression of one group of people by another. This was not done in the manner of realistic, engaged drama, but by means of a metaphysical experience which shattered the control of the old myths over the perceptions of the audience by demonstrating their insufficiency in articulating the nature of the real world. For Genet the theater was a means of revealing the irrational and unfounded nature of these mythical structures.

In *Deathwatch*, the first and most realistic of Genet's plays, Lefranc struggles against the established order of things in order to transcend his demeaning role as a small-time criminal and to become like his fellow prisoner, Yeux-Verts. Lefranc murders his cell mate, Maurice, in hopes of gaining the mask of "Le Vengeur," but he does not realize until too late that such a change in status is more than a matter of volition. Yeux-Verts's position amounts to a calling as he explains to Lefranc: "You don't know anything about

---

[4] "When I was in school, that is from the time I was six until I was twelve or thirteen, the 'East,' and thus 'Islam,' was always presented in French schools . . . as a kind of shadow of Christianity. I, as a little Frenchman, lived in the light. Everything that was Muslim was in a shadow, in the shadow in which I placed Islam ever since the crusades. Do you see? I was conditioned in a way by my French Christian education." (1987, 76).

bad luck if you think you can ask for it. I didn't want mine. It chose me" (53).

Yeux-Verts has his position ratified by the near-deity Boule de Neige: "All the men in his cell acknowledge him. Those in the cells around and the whole fort, and all the prisons in France. He shines, he gives off rays . . . nobody can beat him" (14). The nature of the dominant order is not made explicit but its existence and power manifest themselves in a pattern of hierarchical relations. Boule de Neige is the highest ranking member of the criminal hierarchy. Everyone defers to him, even the prison guards. His influence invests his most insignificant gesture with meaning. Lefranc is trapped at the bottom of the hierarchy. He must be what others say he is. He must accept what R. D. Laing calls his "attributed identity."

Genet's unique vision of the world and the place of the individual in it is obviously congenial to the work of R. D. Laing where one finds many references to the characters and situations in Genet's plays and novels. It is clear that— unlike many literary critics–Laing sees through the facade of the underworld, the small time punk and of the oppressed finding in Genet situations of universal significance. In order to call attention to what is universal— and to my mind— the mythical and ritual nature of Genet's plays, I shall refer frequently to Laing's *Self and Others*.

A person entrapped in an identity which he cannot or will not accept, says Laing, has recourse to "elusion," i.e. entertaining fantasies of being another person (45-46). Unable to realize his desires, Lefranc, like the individual described by Laing, seeks refuge in fantasy. However, he betrays his fantasies and thereby himself. Anticipating Yeux-Vert's imminent execution, Lefranc imagines himself the future lover of his cell mate's widow. Yeux-Verts finds out and warns him against aspiring to be what he is not. "In order to fill my hide, you have to be my size. To be my size, you have to do what I do," which is having a murder to one's credit (40-41). Lefranc's murder of Maurice results from a misunderstanding of Yeux-Verts's words. To be Yeux-Verts is not a matter of volition, i.e., of authentic behavior, but of passivity and absence of self. Yeux-Verts acquired his rank because he committed a murder, not by choice, but because he was impelled to do it by a force greater than himself. It is that same force which provides him with honors and privileges in prison. As Laing points out, once certain attributes have been meted out, they cannot be easily put aside, because they have the force of "injunctions"— the individual is expected to conform to his attributes whether he likes it or not (151). Lefranc does not understand, until it is too late, that social roles are imposed from without, not earned.

Even though we see Lefranc as an ill-fated loser, he is a special, possibly superior, person if only because he perceives that his own identity and the one attributed to him by society are two different things. A person's identity, according to Laing, is attributed to him because the group defines his relation to it as well as his personal characteristics. Unlike Lefranc, most people passively— unconsciously— accept these attributed characteristics which form each individual's "sense of his own agency, perceptions, motives, intentions" (151). There is no room for acts of volition, such as Lefranc's, because they disturb the preordained unfolding of the social ritual. To attempt to assert oneself by sidestepping the hierarchical order is to be automatically excluded from its rituals— or worse, to be made its victim.

"By complimentarity," says Laing, "I denote that function of personal relations whereby the other completes or fulfills self" (82). In *The Maids*, the mistress cannot legitimize her identity without the maids. In turn, the identity of the maids is derived from their mistress. For her part, Madame demands wholehearted confirmation of her attributes as mistress and those of the maids as maids. A situation that would be truly satisfactory for Madame would require the collusion of the maids, that is, they would have to act as though the attributes of maid and mistress were authentic.

Madame wants to be perceived as loving and generous, even though she is totally insensitive to her maids whom she treats like objects. "She loves us like her couches. And more! Like the pink faience of her johns. Like her bidet" (33). And, even though the maids are sisters, Madame does not allow them to address one another familiarly,"In front of her, we can't even talk like we know one another" (74).

Naturally, the maids resent their roles and their lack of sincerity is obvious in the proper, but unloving way they perform them. Madame is exasperated: "Your kindness annoys me. It wears me out. It suffocates me. Your kindness which after so many years never was able to become truly affectionate" (59).

If Madame sounds a bit like a frustrated theatrical director, it is probably not an accident. The topos "All the world's a stage" certainly applies to Genet's (and Laing's) understanding of how the world operates. On stage and off, roles must be performed properly or the desired effect is lost. If most of life is a carefully orchestrated sham, then the truth can be perceived only when the actors fail to perform perfectly, thereby letting the audience catch a glimpse of reality between the cracks in the façade.

In *The Maids*, Genet reveals these cracks by constantly crossing the threshold between illusion and reality, belief and disbelief. Genet disorients the spectator by opening with a play-within-the-play which takes up almost a third of the performance. Only gradually does it become evident that the two women are not really mistress and servant. The tone is false. Their behavior is too extreme and the language too direct. And there are many mistakes: those playing the maids are instructed to give the impression of being maladroit and of forgetting their lines. In a similar manner, Claire and Solange, playing maid and mistress, perform their roles ineptly. When we see the play for the first time, we realize only gradually that the maids are playacting as they forget their lines and lapse occasionally into their everyday roles, and, even more revealing, permit their true feelings to surface briefly.

In ends as well as means, Genet's method is comparable to that of the Noh theater concept of *yugen*. The actor— in the Noh drama and in *yugen* as in Genet's plays— does not seek to convince us that he is in fact the character he is performing. In Noh drama an old man can play the role of a young woman, because he is not expected to become a convincing young woman on the stage; instead, he seeks to give the characteristics an existence of their own (Keene 28-31). Genet had something similar in mind when he suggested that Claire and Solange be played by men. His desire to dissociate the characteristics attributed to a certain category of persons from the persons themselves is also evident in his response to the actor who asked him to write a play about blacks: "But, what is a black? And, for starters, what color is it?" (11). *The Maids* is not about maids, just as *The Blacks* is not about blacks, but about all of us (11). The visionary denounces the sham and hypocrisy of society, but Genet, the dramatist and healer of souls, proposed something more novel: to heal the individual by destroying the mask and thereby liberate the authentic person hidden behind it. The actor goes beyond individual personality traits and conjures up a metaphysical vision of the archetypal character being performed. Thus, the actors are expected to give the impression that their acting is flawed in order to magnify the distinction between the actor and the role being performed, in order to point to the authentic being behind the mask.

Even if the stage characters never become fully aware of their situation, it is impossible for the spectator to ignore it. Genet superimposed upon the "naturalness" of everyday behavior a metaphysical dimension which makes its hidden motives blatantly and unavoidably obvious. (Naturalness is used here in the sense given it by Henri Bergson in his study of laughter— this connection will be explained later in the discussion of *The Balcony*.)

In the first part of the play, the maids perform a litany of abuse against Madame in search of vicarious relief from their oppressive situation. By directing our attention to the struggle between the functions of mistress and servant and away from the specific problems of the maids, Genet focused on the mythical and ritual aspects of their functions. The functions of maid and mistress attain a reality of their own, independent of the persons who carry them out. At the same time, their unintended outbursts of rage, anger and hatred make us aware of the suffering of the maids as human beings whose own lives have been totally deformed by their condition. Claire and Solange take turns in assuming Madame's privileges. They wear the finery they both covet. The ritual is a rehearsal of their intended murder of Madame and it is an opportunity for them to make explicit the suspicion and contempt implicit in her attitude and behavior toward them.

An undercurrent of competition between Claire and Solange manifests itself because they both love the young milkman. So powerful is the competition that Solange/Claire, who begins the ritual vilification of Madame, forgets herself and also abuses her sister, Claire, who in turn must remind Solange of their purpose:

SOLANGE: What?
CLAIRE: Claire, Solange, Claire.
SOLANGE/CLAIRE: Do you think you can steal the beauty of the sky and deprive me of it? Choose your perfumes, your powders, your nail polishes, silk, velvet, lace, and deprive me of it? And take the milkman . . . His youth, his freshness, they bother you, don't they? Admit it, the milkman. To hell with you! . . . Ah! yes,
CLAIRE: Claire! Claire!
SOLANGE/CLAIRE: Ah! yes, Claire. To hell with you! (24-25)

The recognition that these are Madame's maids playacting calls into question all that has been said or has gone before. To whom do the words belong? To whom are they directed? By means of this ambivalent situation, Genet created a metaphysical complement to what might otherwise have been a rather banal game between two idle maids. In the metaphysical revelation which follows, he explored not only the relation between servant and mistress, but also the spiritual infection which such a relation injects into the private lives of the participants.

Claire/Madame's first words are filled with hate which seems to come from both Claire and Madame: "And these gloves! These eternal gloves! I've told you often enough to leave them in the kitchen. Doubtless, it's with this that you plan to seduce the milkman" (13). The contempt for the maids is Madame's; the reference to the milkman concerns the sexual competition between the two sisters.

In a world where everyone plays at being what one is not— whether mistress or servant— it is impossible to love. Both maids desire the milkman, but Claire/Madame voices the fear that "That ridiculous young milkman despises us" (15). Where people treat one another as objects there can be no allowance for human feelings. To determine what is real and what is false is impossible. Love is indistinguishable from exploitation. And, because society cruelly scorns those who permit themselves to be deceived, it is imperative to avoid exposing oneself.

Madame permits herself to interpret the privileges of economic superiority as quasi-divine attributes: "Through me. The maid exists through me alone" (22). The relation between Madame and her maids cannot be justified in human terms. However, Genet found a warped justification for this pathological social relationship whose pattern is repeated in all of his plays— in terms of a mythical and ritual relation between semidivine superior beings and those they dominate. Madame could not exist without her maids.

The maids do not even consider the possibility of an authentic existence; like Lefranc, Warda and Diouf, they cannot even conceive of the possibility of change except in terms of the system which holds them in thrall. Far from rebelling because they want to be delivered from a despised oppressor, the maids desire nothing more than to assume a position similar to

Madame's; they seek the attributes associated with a more exalted position, not freedom. Like Lefranc, the maids merely dream of a new identity as false as the one which oppresses them. Claire commits suicide by drinking the tea intended for Madame so that Solange may escape for both of them. As Solange says, looking forward to their new identity, "Now we are Madame Solange Lemercier. The Lemercier woman. La Lemercier. The famous criminal" (90). Instead of escape and freedom, the struggle of Claire and Solange leads to a new, equally dead, function within the existing system of oppression. Claire chooses to die, but her death is futile because it changes nothing. Instead of the affirmation of humanity, there is the victory of death and the negation of reality.

The Balcony illustrates what Laing calls "collusive" relationships. Collusion involves relationships previously discussed, but with the difference that the parties involved accept their attributions and participate in the complementary relationships that result. Collusion, Laing says, has "resonances of playing at and deception" (108). People agree to behave and look upon one another in a certain manner as long as they benefit from the arrangement. Each one "plays the other's game, though he may not necessarily be fully aware of doing so. An essential feature of the game is not admitting that it is a game" (108).

Of course, Laing was describing the kinds of relationships that occur in the world we live in, the so-called real world. In Genet we find the same relationships as seen from the perspective of art; they are commented upon, analyzed, and judged, but it is up to the spectator to arrive at his or her own conclusions. *The Balcony* is set in a brothel, a very high class house of illusion, which clearly represents the entire world. Outside, in the very neighborhood where the brothel is located, a revolution is taking place; its objective is to overthrow a world which itself is run like an enormous brothel. In the end, the revolutionaries fail because they are seduced by the forces of fantasy and illusion, but not until

Genet delivered a forceful moral essay on freedom, the nature of power and those who wield it.

The anonymous clients of the brothel come to indulge in their fantasies of domination and power and are known only by the roles they play— Judge, Bishop, and General. The Police Chief is another regular visitor, but because he possesses real power and has no need for authenticity to satisfy through fantasy, he does not come for the same reason as the others; he comes because he loves and is loved by Irma, the owner of the brothel. The Police Chief also waits for someone to ask to imitate him and thereby confirm his power. However, the clients, more interested in prestige and the appearance of power, not its essence, prefer more glamorous roles. Unwittingly, the Police Chief looks forward to the day when the freedom, conferred on him by his power, is destroyed because he too must conform to the attributes associated with his position.

The Bishop, for example, unsure of himself, is always fussing with petty details of appearance and posture: "miters, ribbons, golden fabrics, small glassware, genuflections" 22). A fundamental question: How can one be a bishop, or any of the other figures, without being born one? is not asked, but implied. The Bishop, like Lefranc, yearns to break the fetters which bind him to a meaningless everyday existence. But for him, as for Lefranc, such an escape is impossible. However, the effect of the Bishop's preoccupation with his role is to emphasize the metaphysical distinction between self and function.

Before the Bishop can satisfactorily complete his reflections, Irma interrupts to demand payment because the rebels are approaching the house of illusion. It may soon be too late for the clients to get home safely. But the Bishop insists on discussing the functions of the bishop and the sacrifices of authenticity it entails:

> . . . in order to become a bishop, I had to struggle not to be one, but to do that which led to it. Having become bishop, in order to be one, it was necessary . . . that I not cease being aware that I am one in order to fulfill my function. (21)

But the attributes of Bishop, Judge and General cannot stand alone. The Bishop needs his penitent, the Judge a thief, and the General a mare, and this is where the prostitutes come in. "The girls in the brothel," wrote Laing, "are shown to be, in a literal sense, prostitutes. They stand for (pro-stare) whatever the client requires them to be, so that he can become for a while who he wishes to be" (112). The client playing the Judge, for example, pleads with the woman assigned to him to be a proper thief. "Listen, you have to be a model thief if you want me to be a model judge. Fake thief, I'm a fake judge" (30). What never occurs to Lefranc or to the maids is obvious in *The Balcony*: that, as in the outside world, the verisimilitude of a function can be threatened by even a single recalcitrant. The system cannot exist without the adherence and support of the oppressed.

> My existence as judge is an emanation of your being a thief. You only have to refuse to be what you are . . . for me to cease to exist . . . for me to disappear, evaporate. Finished. Turned into thin air. Annihilated. (38)

When the Bishop is called upon to serve in the stead of the real bishop who has been killed by the rebels, he continues to be concerned primarily with playing his role properly. It is now a matter of following the directions of the Photographer: "You don't know how to set yourself up for prayer? Well, at the same time, face God and the lens: Hands together. Head raised. Eyes lowered. That's the classic pose" (189).

Through the monologues of the Bishop and the instructions of the Photographer, Genet fixed our attention upon the irrepressible human yearning to be real, living, puissant. This yearning is not expressed by the actors— after all— they are playing roles; neither they nor the characters they are playing are supposed to be aware of the falsity of the roles they are playing and the lives they lead. However, it is the spectator who must recognize for herself, or himself, that true, authentic existence demands freedom from mechanical, lifeless behavior which results from trying to live life according to a set of ill-fitting attributes imposed from without.

The system is so fragile that Irma must constantly police her employees and her clients to prevent even the slightest smile or joke. "As a matter of fact, I'm against joking. A burst of laughter, or even a smile can knock everything to the ground. Where there is a smile, there is doubt" (63). Laughter, the liberating by-product of Genet's comic vision, exposes, even causes, the cracks in the mask and demystifies, thus breaking its spell. The humor is there to liberate the spectator, for although *The Balcony* is often an amusing play, its ill-fated revolutionaries are humorless, lacking the one weapon which is crucial to their victory.

In *The Balcony*, Genet turned Bergson's theory of laughter on its head. Bergson conceived of all social interaction as an infinitely extensive and elastic ritual. The object of laughter, as Bergson saw it, is to chastise and bring into line the individual who has somehow gotten out of step, whose participation in the ritual of society seems more mechanical than natural (116). In Genet, the mechanical and lifeless is ascribed to society, and the situations and characters of his plays are a dramatic portrayal of these conditions. The character who is out of step is the healthiest. Laughter is a means of chastising the individual who has surrendered to a lifeless existence wearing a mask and acting according to attributes prescribed by society.

Laing ended his lengthy analysis of *The Balcony* unsure of where Genet stood. "Genet leaves it an open question whether or not, or in what sense, there can ever be anything other than collusive make-believe" (117). On the contrary, I find in the play an undercurrent of optimism which is confirmed by the later plays which were not available when Laing was writing *Self and Others*: this is the sense that the playwright can heal his audience by making it aware of the specious nature of the racial and political myths which justify the oppression of one group of people by another.

The Blacks is an exorcism as are all of Genet's plays; however, it is not intended for the liberation of blacks alone, but their oppressors as well. The most dangerous spirits associated with blacks lurk in the unconscious mind of the spectator. In *The Blacks* Genet creates a metaphysical struggle in which whites and blacks, hidden behind the masks of racial and racist identity, confront each other as superhuman forces. Written for an all-black cast, the play calls for the actors to wear white masks while playing members of the Court: the Queen, the Governor, the Judge, the Missionary and the Valet. In addition to their costumes, those who play blacks wear invisible masks of blackness which incarnate the racist's image of the black as well as the racist's self image. Unlike Genet's previous plays in which escape is sought through the imitation of oppressive authority figures, the blacks embrace the characteristics attributed to them. "The blacks blacken themselves," says Archibald, as he exhorts his fellow blacks to maximum collusion with the forces of oppression: "That they persist to the point of folly in being what they are condemned to be, in their ebony, in their odor, in the yellow eye, in their cannibalistic tastes" (66).

In giving substance to the disparate attributes associated with white stereotypes of blacks, Genet made the audience uncomfortably aware of how imperfectly they serve to describe the characters on the stage. As Archibald says to the white court: "We are what you want us to be, and we will be that until the absurd end" (179-180). By pushing their racial identity to its most absurd literal expression, the blacks break the narcissistic spell which has transfixed whites and blacks in poses of mortal enmity.

The attributes of the Blacks are many and contradictory. Blacks are savage, like wild animals, sensual and sexy. They drive Cadillacs and tremble in the face of white superiority. In the jungles the blacks inhabit, even the plants are dangerous. They indulge in magic midnight dances. Their women are the white men's whores, and the white women are the black men's whores. Just as Madame cannot tell Solange from Claire, because she sees them as interchangeable objects contained in the category of maids, "Whites," says Village, "have trouble telling one black from another" (81). As the Valet reminds the blacks: "Think of the difficulty I have in seeing you as humans" (60).

Archibald explains to the audience that the impossibility of communication beyond the limits of racial preconceptions is accepted by the blacks as the basis for their performance:

> Rest assured that a play like this doesn't have a chance of penetrating your precious lives, we will continue to have the politeness, learned among you, to make communication impossible. We will add to the original distance separating us with our displays, our manners, our insolence— for we are also actors. (19)

Of course, Archibald is telling only a partial truth: the actors will not only preserve, but enlarge the distance between themselves and the audience, not for the purpose of collusion, however, but to make it impossible.

What Archibald describes as a harmless performance is meant to subvert the ritual expectations of the whites: the whites assume that it is only natural that the black man should rape and kill the white woman, but the long-delayed, drawn out re-enactment of the white woman's murder proves nothing more or less than the complicity of the audience. On the level of the confrontation between the whites and the blacks, the murder of a white woman is not inevitable, but it has already been committed. The play is a celebration of the murder and, by extension, the racial attributes which it confirms. Without the murder there would be no proof that the blacks are blacks. And without blacks there would be nothing special or superior in being white. The pretense of the blacks, that they are re-enacting the murder of the white woman, is a decoy which serves to bring into the open what the whites prefer to ignore, their own blood lust.

In the re-enactment of the murder, Village recounts how he approached the white woman only to be accused by Neige of desiring her. "In your hatred for her there was an element of desire, therefore of love" (28). (Village suggests that the white woman humiliated him before he killed her. Later, he says she desired him, "because my thighs fascinated her . . . ask her" (92). The tinge of sexual desire in Village for the white woman and in her for him exists, in part, to satisfy the whites. Bobo, the white woman, is a tramp who, normally, would be unworthy of notice by members of the court, but as a victim of the blacks, she becomes worthy of "solemn rites." The Governor finds the scene in which the white woman, played by Diouf, yields to Village's advances, natural. "The woman's giving in. Say what you will, those lads are fine fuckers" (113). The sexual innuendo and the desire for blood become almost palpable as the conflicting testimony puts even the white woman's existence in question. Neige reminds Village of his previous testimony that he found the white woman seated at her sewing machine. Village contradicts himself saying that she was standing behind her counter. From a homeless, smelly tramp, the white woman becomes a worker and a homemaker with a mother to care for. She is described in so many ways that the Court and the audience become impatient because they insist on having their victim, even as they realize that she may not exist at all.

Finally, when it is revealed that there is no body, the Judge protests: "But if there's no body at all, that could kill us" (143). Likewise, the Court feels offended and betrayed by the blacks whom it trusted to live up to the attributes of blackness. Just as Madame, in *The Maids*, requires two inferior creatures in exchange for her generosity, the whites wish to exchange their beneficence for proof that they are indeed dealing with a savage race. As in *The Balcony*, the authority figures all require blacks **that possess black attributes** to justify their existence. The jury needs a murderer. The Queen needs a criminal to pardon. The Missionary needs a criminal to baptize before his savage soul is dispatched to the other world by the authorities (144-145). The blacks, however, refuse to supply the body and thereby complete the circle of collusion. The narcissistic fascination with the mask of the black is broken and, with it, the acceptance of the previous relation between self and other. The oppressor may still have the power to enforce the *status quo ante*, but the laughter of the blacks is the signal that the revolution is at hand.

In Genet's final play, *The Screens*, which was inspired by the Algerian revolt against French colonial rule, revolution is only a pretext to celebrate the appearance of the precursor of freedom: Saïd. For Saïd the struggle is over long before the fighting ends because he has accepted himself as he is without illusions, without narcissistic images to enthrall him. *The Screens* is a complex play; it is about more than just Saïd and his family; it is a recasting and a re-evaluation of the ritual forms found in the preceding plays.[5] Most of the characters in *The Screens*— the colonials, the soldiers of both sides, and some of the prostitutes, such as Warda and Kadidja— have surrendered totally to the masks they carry or covet. The colonials and their military defenders watch as their world and the images it supports disintegrates, but at the same time, are consoled by the victory of the masks they leave behind.

Before being overrun by the native forces, the colonial troops put on one last display of their civilization's military beauty in order to infect the enemy with the desire to imitate them. Brought to the edge of destruction by a narcissistic preoccupation with their image of colonial superiority, the colonials realize that success in infecting the Arabs with their values will be a form of victory. With this in mind, the Lieutenant charges his men to shine even in defeat:

> so that the image you offer to the rebels be of such great beauty, that the image they have of themselves is incapable of resisting. Defeated. It will

---

[5] White points out that in their evolution Genet's plays moved from *The Maids*, which is an "economical and tightly written" play in the fashion of Racine, to *The Screens*, which is "more Shakespearean ... with its interweaving plots, its blend of comedy and tragedy and its political and historical overtones." The visit in 1955 of the Peking Opera to Paris, according to White, contributed to Genet's repertoire of theatrical modes (559).

fall in pieces. Smashed. Or like ice: melted. Victory over the enemy:
morale. (158)

Thus, though they win the battles, the Arab guerrillas are defeated because they adopt the illusions of the colonials.

The denial of self, love of the other, and the affirmation of differences are essential to the collusive relationships which provide the albeit unstable underpinning for racism and colonialism according to Albert Memmi. In his *Portrait of the Colonizer and the Colonized* Memmi duplicated Laing's work with individuals, families and small groups on the level of nation and race. The colonized person's acceptance of the characteristics attributed to him is necessary to the colonizer, because these differences are "excuses without which the behavior of the colonizer would seem scandalous" (109). Once it is accepted by all parties that differences do exist, then there is no possibility of assimilation or compromise. To the mind of the colonizer, although not necessarily that of the oppressed individual, change is impossible because these attributes of inferiority are unchangeable: "these differences, finally, properly constitute its essence" (160). In reaction, the oppressed peoples can purge the shame associated with their attributed differences and actually glorify them: this is the prelude to revolt. This is exactly what has lead to the revolt in *The Blacks*. However, another response is possible; the image of the oppressor may be so powerful that, even as revolt spreads, the only objective of the rebels will become, not liberation, but to assume the attributes of the retreating colonial army.

Instead of liberating themselves and their people, the revolutionary troops in *The Screens* interiorize the oppressive system they have opposed. The camaraderie which has prevailed among the rebels— regardless of their previous social functions— is slowly stifled. Infected by "the beauty of the war," the rebels transmit the malady to their countrymen. The departure of the colonials leaves new roles for the natives to play, new attributes with which to smother their humanity, without actually liberating them. Once the rebels begin to perceive themselves as capable of wearing the discarded masks of their former colonial masters, they lose the ability to consider themselves or others as human beings. They begin to treat themselves and their fellow countrymen as objects just as their enemies did before them.

Even though the revolution is subverted by the victors, not everyone loses. Saïd embodies that cruel self-understanding proclaimed by Rimbaud in his poem "Bad Blood": "It is very obvious to me I've always belonged to an inferior race. I can't figure out revolt. My race never rose up except to loot: like wolves after beasts they haven't killed" (7). He accepts himself as he is despite a crushing load of "faults." His lack of illusions about himself and his possibilities is the key to his liberation. With the poverty he has inherited from his mother comes the emancipating power of laughter. As his Mother says: "I am Laughter, but not just any kind: that which appears when everything goes wrong" (149).

Saïd's freedom is the basis of Leila's freely given devotion to him. He accepts her as she is, without possessions and the ugliest of women to be his wife. His behavior towards her, although treacherous and cruel, comes from an unsentimental acceptance of their reality. At first, Saïd considers working in Europe to earn the bridal price for a more attractive woman, but circumstances oblige him to accept himself as he is: too poor and too miserable for the luxury of compensatory fantasies.

Leila's ugliness also frees her from illusion. She is too ugly to be seduced by her own image. Saïd tells her not to hide her ugliness; he wants the entire world to know that she is "the ugliest woman in the world and the least dear: my wife" (144). She joins her husband in a life of crime, treachery and prison until, no longer able to keep up with him, she is deserted by him. Having accepted the cruel truth of reality, both Saïd and Leila avoid the snares of illusion and fantasy. Nevertheless, while Saïd and Leila do not indulge in dreams of romantic love, they share a mutual affection which their relation to reality permits. In *The Blacks*, under similar circumstances, Village cannot escape with Vertu because he cannot free himself. Unlike Vertu, who can claim "I am the only one to have gone to the farthest reaches of shame" (48), Village has not suffered enough to earn his freedom.

Having freed himself from all illusion, even the illusion that destroyed Roger— the pious hope that the world of fantasy can be overthrown— Saïd is tempted by his compatriots to become a hero. He will, they promise, become a hero after the rebels have executed him for betraying them. His image, recast as that of a martyred hero, could be a unifying symbol for the revolution. From among the dead, Saïd's mother shouts to her son not to yield. "Saïd! . . . You're not going to give in? . . . I didn't keep you in my guts just so you'd become one more or less. Saïd!" (257). But Saïd has already answered for himself. He refuses all threats and blandishments, including the promise by the Surveillant to write songs about the beauty and love of Leila.

In the four-tiered final tableau, Genet summarizes not only *The Screens*, but all of his plays. On the top level are the dead whose numbers have been swollen by the fighting. On the other levels, various aspects of life, including the temptation and death of Saïd, take place. This tableau presents a vision of life and death comparable to that of the shaman described by Eliade. It is a world in which:

> *Everything seems possible*, where the dead return to life and the living die only to live again, where one can disappear and reappear instantaneously, where the "laws of nature" are abolished, and a certain superhuman "freedom" is exemplified and made dazzlingly present. (511)

Genet's characters die on one level and reappear on another. While life for many of the dead was a form of hell, death with its laughter and camaraderie is a paradise. In death, there is liberation from the power of the mask; it is the ultimate demystification of the world of illusion and provides the justification for Saïd's behavior. Without the added dimension of the world of the dead, Saïd would be no more than a traitor and a thief. However, the dead prove not only the vanity of choosing sides, but, that making such choices is a betrayal of life and humanity. Saïd's mother comes to the level of the dead with the soldier she has accidentally strangled. The Lieutenant joins Si Slimane and Kadija, but the former enemies show no hate. Without the masks of the oppressor and the oppressed, without illusions of social or economic distinctions, they are mere humans. Saïd's refusal to take sides or to permit himself to be deified is justified as a recognition of the humanity he shares with all men. The world of the living is revealed as the true world of death because of its domination by lifeless masks and rituals; the vision of death, on the other hand, is a metaphysical revelation of the path to resurrection. "The victory over evil and evil men is not punishment, it is not the casting of them into the eternal flames of hell" wrote Nicolas Berdyaev, in a passage appropriate to Genet's eschatological vision, "It is transformation and enlightenment, the dispersal of the phantom world of evil as a delightful nightmare" (144).

The Screens was Genet's last play. Genet was so acutely sensitive to the way people circumscribe one another's freedom that, like Saïd, he turned his back on the world, to possessions, literature, friends. He spent his last years, until his death in 1986, preferring solitude, interrupted by visits to his few friends, as a means of preserving his own freedom and, at the same time, preventing himself from interfering with the freedom of others (Jelloun 29-31). "As soon as I speak," Genet explained to an interviewer, "I am betrayed by the situation, I am betrayed by the person who is listening to me, simply as a function of communication" (1987, 78). Only what he considered a good revolt, a rebellion against oppression— the Palestinian cause, for example— could convince him to leave his solitude and lend his name to support the Palestinian *fedayeen*:

The revolt of each man is necessary. We carry out little rebellions every day. As soon as we make a little disorder— otherwise stated, as soon as we make our own order, an order that is particular, individual to us— we carry out a revolt. (1987, 76)

Chapter Four

Tyranny: A Laboratory for
The Theater of Healing

In 1977 I published an article in *World Literature Today* about Athenian theater during the Greek dictatorship which lasted from 1967 to 1974. Born and raised in the United States, I had never experienced life under a dictatorship, and when I went to Greece in 1973 I found that superficially life was not strikingly different from what it was during my previous stay in 1963-1964. From time to time something would jolt me into remembering that the situation was not normal.

I knew that some of my students were involved in anti-junta activities and that some of them had been imprisoned and mistreated by the police. A young man in one of my literature classes gave up plans to become a jazz musician after he was beaten around the head until his hearing was permanently impaired. In general, though, neither my students nor the general population made a show of resistance, save in exceptional circumstances, such as the funeral of former Prime Minister George Papandreou. In class my students stuck to the business at hand. They could just as well have been in some midwestern American university. One of my American colleagues, a militantly apolitical person, who was teaching T. S. Eliot at the time, kept complaining to me, "These students just don't understand twentieth-century alienation." The fact of the matter was that they not only were aware of their alienation, but many were struggling to bring about a revolution to overcome it.

The only place where revolution was tangibly in the air was in the theaters of Athens. I had heard that in the summer festivals, where classical Greek plays are performed, audiences applauded whenever actors reached a point in a play where references to freedom had been excised by the censor, but I was not prepared to experience a theater where everything seemed to demand a struggle against the oppression. In my article I discussed several plays by Greek dramatists which had made the greatest impression on me. Mainly, I explained the context in which the plays were performed and gave rather extensive summaries of them because they were not available in English. Since 1977 I have continued to think about the significance the theater under the dictatorship and about its connection to the theater of central Europe, a subject about which several articles have been published since the fall of communism in the former Soviet Union.

The questions had to do with the reception of a play by the audience. How can we measure, or determine, the effect of a play on a spectator, or a group of spectators? Under normal circumstances there are too many factors; the theater's "unwieldy polytextuality," as Denis Calandra calls it (14), makes it difficult, if not impossible, to measure audience response. However, theater in special circumstances, where the oppressive practices of a dictatorship have focused the feelings and needs of the people by closing out other, normal paths of expression and desire, create a laboratory for the study of audience reception. Here, instead of theoretical speculation about audience response, we have concrete, if not clinical proof of the efficacy of the theater. There is even proof that theater does heal the psychic wounds caused by an oppressive regime, and that the communal experience it provides helps the individual overcome the sense of alienation from self and society. That it is the source of a catharsis, as Jauss describes it, in "which the imagination, stirred by affects and set free, can act" (96). Jauss does not specify what kind of action can result, but we can see in the examples provided by the experience of the theater under tyranny that it can not only provide the sense of self identity, of individuality, that we find in Genet, or the political orientation sought by Brecht, but it can actually inspire and lead the audience to move its quest for individual and political freedom into the streets.

The situation in Czechoslovakia which led to the Velvet Revolution in 1989 has many parallels to the one in Greece in 1973. In comparing the case of the Greek theater to that of the Czech theater we find a certain pattern is repeated. The imposition of dictatorial rule, which includes censorship and the attempt to control the thoughts and behavior of the population, renders traditional forms of theater meaningless. In normal times, people go to the theater for a variety of reasons, from a desire to be entertained, enlightened, or simply to improve one's status through a visible association with one of the arts. But in times of tyranny the theater audience seems to be of one mind; it needs to be reminded of its collective love of freedom and to be spiritually armed for resistance. The change of political context brings about a change in the taste and needs of the audience which can be satisfied only by an indirect, allusive, non-realistic form of drama which deals with inner states of being, and not the illusion of realistic theater that suggests we are prying into another person's mind or peeking into his bedroom.

First let us look at the case of the Greek theater during the dictatorship of the colonels. When, after the *coup d'état* in 1967, strict censorship was imposed on the traditionally lively Athenian theater, there seemed little possibility of its being revived as long as the junta remained in power. What actually happened was that, after a period of readjustment, the theater reappeared metamorphosed in response to the political climate. In its new guise the theater became one of the principle forms of anti-junta resistance. The need to find a proper response, one in which its themes were opaque to the censors, but transparent to the audience, played a greater role in determining the nature of the Greek theater during the final years of the dictatorship than the idiosyncrasies of individual playwrights, the traditional preferences of the audience and a theoretical orientation toward the ideas of Piscator and Brecht.

These playwrights created new mythical figures representing the oppressive situation. Common to all of these plays are the themes of oppression, betrayal, the desire for freedom, anguish, helplessness, revolt. Although some of the plays find their subject matter in analogous situations in Greek history and folklore, their protagonists usually do not have the unique, individualistic traits common to realistic drama; instead they are typical, Everyman characters representative of the people sitting in the audience.

Despite their obvious debt to contemporary Western dramatic theory and to the models of their Central European counterparts, the Greek playwrights of this period did more than imitate foreign models. Each work bears the individual stamp of the dramatist's imagination and talent as well as the influence of the censor. In addition, the immense popularity of these plays during the time of the dictatorship and only then is proof of a transformation in the Greek theatergoer's sensibility.

There is little room here to discuss reasons for the dictatorship, except to say that it proved a tragic disappointment to its supporters and a source of unmerited pain for its opponents. In the repressive means used to establish and maintain its power, the junta resembled that of its fellow tyrants to the north. The rhetoric of the colonels earned them the epithet "clowns" from Constantine Karamanlis, the former prime minister of Greece who was destined to pick up the pieces in 1974, after they provoked the catastrophic Turkish invasion of Cyprus and brought their unprepared country to the brink of war.

The junta took over Greece on April 21, 1967, with the jingoistic slogan "Greece of Christian Greeks." They announced they were saving Greece from an imminent communist take-over by which they meant a government under Andreas Papandreou. They made the standard promises to clean up the government and make the trains run on time. Instead, they put their cronies in key positions and made sweetheart contracts with local and foreign businessmen. As proof of their anti-communism they arrested thousands of old men who had been considered security risks in the late 1940s during the Greek Civil War. When they realized that the old men in the concentration camps on Makronisos posed no danger, they were released and replaced with younger people newly designated as subversives. They attempted to revive artificial puristic Greek which had been dying a natural death because the Greeks preferred to use the demotic Greek they spoke at home and in their everyday affairs. Colonel George Papadopoulos' speeches and those of his lieutenants, such as Stylianos Pattakos, purportedly in puristic Greek, were absurdly nonsensical and a source of humor, and more than anything proved the foolishness of any further attempts to replace the spoken language with an artificial one. Although the American government denied it was involved in the coup, there was a general belief held both by opponents and supporters of the dictatorship, that it had the blessing of Washington. Members of the junta and their supporters were not averse to telling Greeks "We are the Americans." The regular visits of then Vice President Spiro Agnew to Athens reinforced this impression.

Unfortunately, the behavior of the junta was not a laughing matter. Their profligate attempts to buy public support where they could not earn it destroyed the economy which had been so painstakingly built up during the 1950s and 1960s. Although the abuse of human rights in Greece was not as extensive and systematic as in the communist countries, imprisonment and torture for political crimes was common. In the first years of the regime, there was the feeling that the junta had spies everywhere. In short the dictatorship infected Greek society with fear and insecurity; not knowing who to trust, people felt isolated and helpless. The theater provided a means of overcoming this fear and gave people a renewed sense of solidarity. The theatrical performance provided a sublimation, a consolation and, ultimately, was the source of a heightened awareness of common spiritual needs denied by the physical reality to which the Greek was obliged to conform. The communal experience of the theater provided theater-goers with clear evidence that they were not alone in their resistance to the status quo. It provided proof that those who were opposed to the situation, though intimidated by the oppressive policies of the junta, were in the majority.

In the fifties and early sixties, before the imposition of the dictatorship, the Athenian theater offered four basic choices: situation comedies; melodramas; revues with topical satire, music and plump dancers; and, from the West, serious plays. A typical theater season, that of 1963-1964, for example, presented the most successful plays from New York, London and Paris in addition to important revivals. Bolt's *A Man for All Seasons*, Pirandello's *Tonight, We Improvise* and Genet's *The Balcony* were among the imports. In the variety of their interests, Athenian theatergoers resembled their counterparts in any democratic country.

Reflecting the circumstances created by the dictatorship, the taste of Greek theatergoers changed radically. In part, the change is evident in the kind of foreign plays which drew large and enthusiastic audiences. Considering the traits shared by their governments with the Athens regime, it should not be surprising that Central Europe became an important source for new plays. Two of the biggest hits the 1973-1974 season were *Tango* by Polish playwright Slawomir Mrozek and *The Holders of the Keys* by the Czech Milan Kundera. Other plays were Vaclav Havel's *Memorandum* and an adaptation of Jaroslav Hasek's *Good Soldier Schweik*. Pavel Kohout, another Czech, had two plays, *Poor Murderer* and *Augustus, Augustus*, running concurrently.

Many of the plays which came from the West during the same season were part of the dramatic tradition, described by Rosette Lamont, as "metaphysical farce," which inspired the Central European plays. Among these plays were Ionesco's *The Thirst and the Hunger*, Jean-Paul Sartre's *No Exit*, Roger Vitrac's

Victor, or The Children Take Power and two different versions of Jarry's *Ubu Roi*. Some of the plays mentioned above had been previously performed in Greece, but their revival during the 1973-1974 season along with similar plays reinforces the impression that their return was due not to chance, but because they served certain compelling needs of the audience.

The Greeks reacted to the same kind of stimuli as those who had lived under communism, and like them they searched for a form of theater suited to their needs. They sought inspiration and models from many of the same sources. Greek playwrights repeated the experience of the Russian playwright Vasily Aksyonov, who in searching for a new means of theatrical expression, first found it in Ionesco's *Rhinoceros* and *The Chairs* which were circulating in samizdat. Later, Aksyonov says, he discovered Brecht, Slawomir Mrozek and then, in 1965/1966, Beckett's *Waiting for Godot* (20). Research into his own country's theater tradition led him to a 1920s Russian literary group called the Oberiuty, and the "absurd" plays by Kharms and Vvedensky (21). Aksyonov's movement to a non-realistic form of drama was repeated by many artists.

Olga Chtiguel describes a similar movement that gradually involved the entire Czech theater community. The first steps were taken in the 1950s in "off mainstream" theaters whose experiments with non-realistic modes showed the way of resistance to the communist regime. The Theater on the Balustrade, started in 1959, developed a "synthetic theatre which utilized anti-illusionistic acting, minimal stage design, and topical dramaturgy" (91). Gradually more changes came, some initiated by the "auteur's" theater whose acting style "was antipsychological, nonillustrative, and individualistic, deliberately playful, seemingly unpolished, raw, and spontaneous" (92).

In order to get past the censor means had to follow content. This resulted in what Chtiguel calls a "happening":

Stage aesthetics were inspired by visual arts, silent motion pictures, and commedia dell'arte. To stress physicality, visual metaphor, and rhythm in their mise-en-scenes, directors freely explored and combined numerous genres and sources: drama, musicals, vaudeville, melodrama, and cabaret, as well as lectures, meditations, acrobatics, and magicians. (92)

Discussing Eastern European theater in the late 1950s and 1960s, Daniel Gerould summarizes the themes of oppression thus:

the individual at the mercy of the state, the crushing power of bureaucracy, the constant threat of a police mechanism that terrorizes its citizens, the corruption of language and feeling by a system that professes the highest ideals and practices something quite different. (1984, 2)

The same themes are found in the Greek theater during the dictatorship. Gerould speaks of the "centrality of theatre in a culture that is everywhere falsified and manipulated," because it is difficult to control. In a society where the government lies as a matter of course and where citizens lie to one another for self protection, people learn the art of "reading between the lines and discovering hidden meanings, even where none exist." These people become "an, alert hungry audience" ready for "the showman's craft of subterfuge, misdirection, and metaphor" (1984, 4). Such characteristics clearly point to the use of humor. "Eastern European drama," says Gerould, "excels at comedy, parody, sarcasm, the absurd, and the grotesque" (1984, 7), all weapons in the struggle against propaganda of the state.

In the West, playwrights claimed they were inventing new dramatic forms to avoid the bourgeois, establishment theater of a consumerist society; in the East, playwrights refused to look at their bare-shelves society of scarcity through the rose-colored spectacles of socialist realism. In both cases, the protest was against a form of realistic drama which trivializes human needs and feelings, encourages conformity, and seeks to entertain rather than illuminate the spirit.

In a dictatorship, the government assumes the role of playwright. It tells citizens what roles to play and which words to speak. Stepping out of the assigned role or telling the truth is a punishable offence, and thus everyday life becomes a fictional construct, a-play-within-each-life, so to speak, and the longer the situations exists, the more difficult it is to distinguish the play-acting from real life. This kind of confusion contributes, according to Gerould, to the "heightened theatricality" typical of the work of Central European writers and which "springs from the nature of their equivocal relation to reality and pseudo-reality" (1980, 6). The playwright contributes to the healing of society by giving concrete expression to the inner and outer worlds of the spectator. The dramatist thus guides the audience out of the world of make-believe and into the real world.

Like their counterparts elsewhere, Greek dramatists found that to deal with tyranny they had to bring a new form of theater to the Greek stage. In doing so, they found for the first time an eager audience. Evidence of the reorientation of the Greek theater audience was the unprecedented enthusiasm for plays by serious contemporary Greek playwrights. Between 1970 and 1974, over fifty-two new plays by Greek dramatists were produced, something unheard of in modern Greece where audiences normally preferred their "quality" theater to bear a foreign signature. Prominent among the many dramatists whose works were produced during this period are Yorghos Kampanelis, who differs from the others in that he had had several successful plays before 1967, Yorghos Skourtis, Marietta Rialdi and Stratis Karras, whose plays will be discussed here.

Kampanelis' *Our Great Circus*, replete with Brechtian alienation effects, is a series of historical vignettes loosely tied together with songs and placards which underline their common significance. The scenes are set in classical Greece, Byzantium, and in the 1820s, the time of the Greek revolution. Greek history is presented as a ritual repetition of a modern myth whose motifs include internecine strife, revolt and betrayal. In *Our Great Circus* history and myth become one in a recurring nightmare of momentary glory subverted by treachery and transformed into defeat and subjugation. However, regardless of the recurring myth waiting in the wings, there are always brave persons willing to sacrifice themselves in a foredoomed insurrection against oppression. Kampanelis' play provides a dramatic paraphrase of Ernst Cassirer's statement, "The myth of a people does not determine but is its fate" (5). The fruits of victory are snatched from those who do the fighting. They are set aside and forgotten until long after their deaths when they are no longer a threat. Then they are transformed by those who betrayed them into inoffensive symbols of patriotism and statues are raised in their honor.

In the first scene, agents of Philip of Macedon bribe the priests to set up a new Pythia at Delphi in order to secure a favorable oracle against Demosthenes and those who support the idea of uniting the Greek city-states against the outsiders. Romios (the Greek) and Romiaki (the little Greek), the ringmaster-interlocutors who oversee the "circus" and occasionally participate in it, make feverish preparations to receive Philip's agents at Delphi. Romiaki plays the replacement for the High Priestess of Delphi (the old one having been done away with in order to increase the likelihood of oracles favorable to Philip). Romiaki and Romios frequently cross the line between the scenes of "historical" make-believe, and their function with the rest of the audience, as observers . As in the plays of Genet and Brecht, the manipulation of the "real" and the "make-believe" serves to emphasize the recurring, universal context of the situation.

Romiaki is both Romiaki and the High Priestess. Simple soul that she is, she cannot believe that such underhanded skullduggery as she is called upon to perform is possible. She is terrified of being punished by Zeus for impersonating a priestess (until Romios, playing a priest in the pay of the Macedonian, assures her that Zeus too has been bought off), and, at the same time, she fears the consequences of failing her new masters. To bring herself and her nerves under control, the new High Priestess gets drunk and almost bungles her first oracle. Finally, Philip gets what he wants and the High Priestess is the first to give herself to his representatives.

Kampanelis' audiences did not miss the allusion to their own recent political experience. They were sure to associate the corrupt oracle and the contemporary affairs of the Greek Orthodox Church. Both dictators, George Papadopoulos and Dimitris Ioannidis, who overthrew the former, having taken secular affairs into their hands, did not neglect the Greek Church. They had their men "elected" Archbishop of Athens and made certain that the official incense carried prayers on their behalf. It is with these vignettes, where myth and history intersect, that Kampanelis gives expression to the metaphysical reality of the audience. He provides an understanding not unlike the one described by Kitazawa in which "Myth could change reality itself" (174).

Byzantium provides the setting for another scene. A beggar lavishes praise on Andronicus, the usurper of the Byzantine throne, while revealing that Constantinople has been sold piecemeal to "allies" who have acquired port facilities and are greedily preparing for more. The revolutionary heroes of 1821 liberate Greece and, in good faith, greet the new king imposed on them by their "Christian protectors" of the Holy Alliance. They live to see the land they fought for divided among Bavarian fortune hunters and obsequious Greeks who avoided taking up arms during the insurrection. Those who resist too vigorously are permanently disposed of with the guillotine donated by their French protectors. The choice left to the heroes of 1821 is between death and servitude as porters for the rich and powerful.

In the manner of Brecht, Kampanelis "knots" the scenes with songs which summarize the action and focus on its meaning. Underlying each scene are the mythical motifs of Greek history. All mythical heroes must struggle against the crushing forces of nature or, in Kampanelis' case, against the movement of history.

What is reasserted, as each mythical hero takes arms against the forces which will destroy him, is the indomitable nature of humanity. The myth is cyclical because there is always a new hero to rise up against the tyrants, whoever they may be. In the end *Our Great Circus* is redeemed by those who never forget their pride or sell out. Because they renew a foredoomed struggle, Kampanelis gives these heroes a special dignity. By the end of each performance of Kampanelis' play the atmosphere in the theater was one of incipient revolt. In fact, in mid-November 1973, as the audience left the theater, it found an actual revolt taking place in the streets.

Conspiratorial euphoria and camaraderie dominated performances of *Our Great Circus* and of Skourtis' *Karaghiozis, Almost a Vizir*. Whereas Kampanelis uses ancient Greek myth for the basic structure of his play, Skourtis taps the popular folk art of the shadow theater. Its characters with their simple, caricatural personalities are archetypes of the Greek experience. Hadjiavatis is the bearded worshiper of authority and the constant companion of Karaghiozis. Stavrakas is the swaggering, but cowardly, tough who represents the low life of harbor cities. The Turks, including Mustapha Bey, Veligekas and the Vizir, are as powerful and capricious as the forces of nature. Karaghiozis, the Hellenized hero of the Turkish shadow theater, needs all his cunning to survive in a world of injustice and violence. In using traditional folk characters and situations to make a commentary on the present, Skourtis participates in the tradition of sedition typical of shadow theater in Mediterranean countries once part of the Ottoman Empire. The purpose is serious, but the weapon is laughter provoked by the puppetlike characters on the stage, but directed at the repressive regime running the country.

The traditional setting of plays about Karaghiozis presents the palace of the local Turkish dignitary on one side of the screen and Karaghiozis' hovel on the other. Most of Skourtis' play is set in the Vizir's throne room. However, in re-creating the traditional struggle between the haves and the have-nots, Skourtis does not permit us to forget for one moment that Karaghiozis and his friends live their lives in misery and poverty.

Their suffering has left indelible marks on their personalities and physical appearance. Their typically exaggerated gestures, their unmotivated and endless violence, and an atmosphere charged with greed and conspiracy, all recall the puppet-like figures of Jarry's *Ubu roi*. Karaghiozis' hump, the symbol of oppression and countless beatings, and an exceptionally long arm (to provide a longer reach when he is stealing, begging or pummeling one of his sons or Hadjiavatis) describe his nature and condition as vividly as Ubu's pear-shaped frame.

Karaghiozis' adventure begins because the Vizir is beset by his own courtiers who seek to overthrow him. To save his throne he calls upon the ever-ravenous and cunning Karaghiozis and his friends, who through sheer blundering luck manage to drive out the rebels and find themselves the possessors of an empty throne room vacated by the terrified Vizir. Karaghiozis places himself on the throne and discovers its ability to provide him and his party with abundant food. His scepter, quite appropriately, is a large soup ladle (which recalls Jarry's more audacious use of a toilet cleaning brush for the same purpose). Power is the source of food, and Karaghiozis and his cohorts are soon groaning with distended stomachs.

In the meantime, the Vizir, reconciled with his chastened lieutenants, returns to recapture the privileges abandoned to the common people. The unprepared Karaghiozis is as decisive a leader as Ubu when he comes under strong attack. He quickly finds himself dethroned and hungry again. The parallel with the almost bloodless coup of 21 April 1967 is clear. And so is the moral: anyone who wants to hold power must be prepared and willing to fight for it.

Those who cannot hold power must learn to live with it; this is the subject of *Oust*, Marietta Rialdhi's tragic satire. *Oust* opens with the scene of a dreamlike middle-class party. The actors' words are drawn out and meaningless. Naked to the waist,

Eriphili crawls around the small stage while muttering incomprehensibly, an image of the libido humiliated and diverted from its creative mission. The dream becomes a nightmare with the entry of Ok. Wearing a long, double-breasted overcoat, a beard, glasses and a military top, Ok announces that the City has just been saved. Of course everyone is grateful, but beyond that, they are also curious. They would like to know who has been saved and from whom. Ok refuses to go into details.

Ok's function is not clear at first, but slowly we realize that he is the emissary from an invisible playwright. His job is to deliver the new script to the frightened citizens and to assign them roles. The citizen actors are obliged to improvise, because he provides only general guidelines as to what roles they are supposed to play. Although there is a high level of anxiety among the citizens, they also have a certain amount of experience, because there have been other dictatorships and they have played similar roles before.

Almost everyone plays along with a dictatorship, at least some of the time, even if it is only to pretend not to be concerned with its existence. Rialdhi makes the strings obvious and, even though the audience is laughing, it realizes that when it emerges from the theater it will have to put its strings back on. The spectator's sense of derision is turned inward, a signal that this situation cannot go on.

After Ok's departure, there are new efforts to simulate lighthearted gaiety. However, the rather feeble effusiveness evaporates as the guests begin, without reason, to suspect one another of undefined crimes. The party is interrupted a second time by Ok, who is pursuing a fugitive said to be responsible for allegedly threatening to create a disturbance at the railway station. The suspect must be apprehended in order to restore civic calm and confidence in the government. Ok appeals to Xenophon's patriotism and cupidity to stand in for the guilty party. Cooperation with the new regime will mean a short stay in jail, but the City will be saved and a substantial reward will be waiting for Xenophon when he is released from prison. Some of the other guests are induced to testify against him. After the undercover hero has been led to prison, the guests, reviewing the evening's events, come to believe that he is truly guilty.

Adelaïda and Hippocrates, the hosts, decide to play along with the new government, as they did with those which preceded it. They spy on their neighbors and show up at public meetings to applaud the Leader and jeer at those out of favor. They take care of the government and the government takes care of them. As he must, the Leader eventually falls, and the city is rescued by new saviors in search of new scapegoats and collaborators. Accustomed as they are to tyranny, the citizens of the City easily fall into step. Only the young, beautiful Eriphili cannot survive living permanently in a prison state, and the final scene becomes her death rite.

Apart from the obvious political allusions in *Oust*, its effect is to magnify the horror of the mechanism of oppression contained in the play's central myth. Rialdi's characters and their situations are too vague and too changeable to be ascribed to a specific source. At the same time the audience was led to the unavoidable consciousness of its own fears and insecurities in a world where heroes and traitors were manufactured from among its members in order to sustain the organized irrationality of the colonels.

Whereas Rialdi creates a bizarre, dreamlike world whose horror is mitigated by humor, the plays of Stratis Karras engender anguish without relief. In Karras' *The Troupers* there is endless waiting for events which fail to take place and suffering because of unwanted events which do occur. The effect of *The Troupers* is cumulative, a bit like seeing a particularly nasty dream several nights in a row. Karras' characters, performers in a seedy sideshow, earn their insecure living by brutally punishing themselves in order to entertain others. There are two sets of performers with similar acts competing for work from the same impresario. The competition between these characters increases their anguish and leads them to even more self-destructive behavior. Their competitive, insecure status is a gruesome parody of the world of the Greek worker: a world of unemployment and extreme competition for those places which do exist, made even more intolerable by a tyrannical state.

Miltos and Melpos perform short skits in which Melpos impersonates a woman. Miltos is the first to enter the rural café where they have supposedly been hired to perform. When he enters, he is happy, but the café is filled with threatening objects. He finds placards, but cannot tell whether they are for or against the "situation." Their discovery might lead to the cancellation of his performance. Worse yet, he could be punished if he is caught near them. Is it a trap? Obviously there is room for fear, but it cannot be defined or discussed. A blind man rides a bicycle on-stage, but his answers to Miltos' questions only add to the confusion.

Melpos adds his nervous sense of unpreparedness to the scene. He and Miltos must set up the stage and rehearse. Next, Londos, whose gimmick is the systematic devouring of an automobile, comes in with his mother. Londos suffers terribly because digesting automobile parts worsens his ulcer, but it is the only work he knows. The three performers wait with feverish anticipation for the Impresario who engaged them. For all of them, work will mean an end to their suffering.

The impresario never appears. Instead, the blind cyclist returns from time to time to add to their anxiety with his cryptic words. To make matters worse, performers with acts paralleling those of Miltos, Melpos and Londos arrive. They claim to have been hired by the same impresario and boast of their superior talents. Melpos, Miltos and Londos redouble their efforts to impress their employer. The play ends unresolved as the stage lights slowly fade out on the frantic preparations of the six actors.

The Troupers has much in common with *Waiting for Godot*, except that the waiting is accompanied by an anguish maintained at the highest possible pitch. The characters are less realistic than those of Samuel Beckett, or of Skourtis and Rialdhi. They are grotesques whose only reason for existence is to serve as expressions of pain, fear and anguish. It is impossible to identify with the characters, yet the members of the audience are caught up in the cathartic metaphysical revelation of their own feelings of oppression. We experience the characters as emotions, not individuals. In this case the spectator is compelled to fill in the blanks left by the playwright in order to complete the play. As I watched it, I felt a tremendous urge to see a resolution of the dilemma facing the troupers, the dilemma which I was facing; I recognized the pain as my own and knew it had to stop.

Karras and his fellow dramatists create ritual and myth, as Artaud suggested, from the obsessions of their contemporaries. Their abstract characters and situations are expressions of recurring elements in the history of the Greek nation which the military dictatorship only served to accentuate. I can only speculate about the effect of the plays on Greek audiences. It was obvious from the way people thronged to the theater that they found in it something they craved. Consolation for the oppression? A communal reassurance that their resistance to the dictatorship was justified? Courage? Perhaps all of these. In his novel, *The Unbearable Lightness of Being*, Milan Kundera describes "lightness" as a spiritual quality of twentieth-century humanity, the feeling that the individual counts for nothing in our overpopulated world of mass movements. Kundera's narrator, trying to survive and understand the end of the Prague Spring, is particularly susceptible to this sense of lightness, yet the novel reassures the reader of the value of each person's life. It restores our sense of "heaviness," of individual value and importance. In a similar manner, the Greek theater of the early seventies served as an antidote to the lightness of being resulting from several years of living in a police state. It is the sense of being part of a lifeless mechanism, the blight which settled on Greek life, a deadening of the individual sense of worth. If it is possible to gauge the atmosphere which prevailed in Greece during the dictatorship, surely the plays I have discussed provide an accurate measurement of it. While they provided a reflection of the time, they also served as its antidote.

In Czechoslovakia, according to Chtiguel, the theater had a salutary effect. Not only did it show the Czech people how to survive the oppression and sterility of Communism, she says, but was instrumental in its overthrow: "the words spoken from the theatre stages did move the masses and changed the course of history" (94). Kitazawa claims that in Poland, Jerzy Grotowski's plays brought about a "change of reality" which "influenced people in Poland deeply enough to be part of what overthrew the socialist regime" (171).

Petr Oslzy, writing about the Velvet Revolution which started on November 17, 1989, describes it as "the most momentous fusion of theatre and society in the entire history of world theatre." People of the theater, students and others joined to lead a united "nation's struggle against the despotism of the totalitarian system" (97). When the strike ended, communism had fallen. Not only did the theater contribute to the spirit of the revolt, according to Oslzy, but the revolt itself took on the aspect of a theatrical event:

> the "velvet revolution" itself shared many features with the theatre. A delicate theatrical quality could be seen in so many situations. And at times the revolution was transformed into a carnival. And perhaps that was one of the deepest reasons it was called the velvet revolution. In the theatre, real blood never flows. (108)

Unfortunately, as the Greeks discovered, when the theater overflows its bounds, there is no guarantee that blood will not flow as well. In November 1973 students in Athens, Patras, Thessaloniki and Ioanina started a revolt that, had it succeeded, might have served as a prototype for the Velvet Revolution. In Athens students occupied the Polytechnion and set up a clandestine transmitter calling on all Greeks to revolt against the dictatorship. Ham radio operators retransmitted the program of the Polytechnion station and soon it was impossible to walk the street of Athens without hearing the previously banned music of Mikis Theodorakis and the appeals of the students. The authorities did not intervene immediately, giving the impression that they lacked the will to act and the streets around the Polytechnion began to fill with people. It was as though an enormous city-wide Happening were taking place. There were somgs, posters and banners calling for the downfall of the junta, processions carrying effigies. Buses and automobiles passing through the crowd were decorated with revolutionary slogan and sent off to spread the revolt. By the night of November 16th, the crowd stretched as far as Omonia and Academia Squares. On Leoforos Alexandras buses and trucks were commandeered to blockade the streets. Again, even though armored riot control vehicles had moved to the edges of the crowd and tear gas filled the air, the authorities seemed hesitant to act. For many this was proof that dawn would find democracy restored. That evening, after having wandered alone in the crowd for several hours, I returned home about midnight and sat in bed with my radio tuned in to the student program. While I was listening to the increasingly confident and triumphant announcements of the speakers, I heard a rumbling coming from the direction of the Greek Defense Ministry which is in the Papagos neighborhood several kilometers from the Polytechnion. My apartment was located between the two. As the rumbling became stronger I realized that a column of tanks was heading for the Polytechnion. By morning, when I returned to the Polytechnion the walls of the school were a shambles. Small groups of young people were still in the streets taunting the soldiers and police who would charge them accompanied by armored vehicles whenever too many of them gathered in one place. According to the historian Richard Clogg, there were at least thirty deaths. "Although the students were crushed by overwhelming force," he says, "their action helped precipitate the overthrow of Papadopoulos" by Dimitrios Ioannidis, the commander of the military police (167). Afterward, many felt that Ioannidis purposely permitted the revolt to get out of hand so he could justify the violence used to crush it and his own coup against Papadopoulos a few days later, a reminder that in a tyranny the state often remains the ultimate playwright.

With the fall of the dictatorship in 1974, the needs of the audience changed. The restoration of democracy in Greece brought about the abolition of most forms of censorship and resulted in a crisis in the theater. Theaters, which had enjoyed a large and growing patronage, suddenly found themselves empty. Audiences became unpredictable once again and sought variety where previously they could only be satisfied with variations on the theme of oppression.

For obvious reasons, "the anti-Communist repertoire . . . lost its appeal" following the Velvet Revolution in Czechoslovakia and the theater there experienced a similar loss of public interest.. Chtiguel suggests, more hopefully than anything, that the Czech theater will find a new healing role in "the repair of damaged souls"(95). On the other hand, Oslzy says that the Velvet Revolution did away with the need many felt for the theater. "Those who came to these theatres were people who in a normal democratic society would be interested in things other than the theatre" (101). The theater gave people what they could find nowhere else. Perhaps it is too optimistic to assume that they would return to the theater with their previous fervor once control of their own lives was restored to them.

The return of democracy led to a new metamorphosis in the Greek theater. The 1975-1976 Athenian theater season saw the comeback of the revue. The dictatorship and the new political situation provided ample material for their satirical skits. The revues had a backlog of previously forbidden material to perform. Playwrights, such as Kampanelis and Skourtis, however, were still looking for their bearings in the new situation. Kampanelis' *The People Are the Enemy*, although it drew large crowds attracted by the playwright's reputation, a musical score by the hitherto banned Mikis Theodorakis and a first-rate cast, lacked the power of *Our Great Circus*. The social and political situation can be blamed for part of the lessened audience response, but, once possessing the freedom to be more realistic and to appeal directly to the intellect, Kampanelis might be said to have neglected his ability to touch the emotions. Likewise, Skourtis' *The Strike*, with its simplistic, agitprop construction, its openly Marxist line, was only a boring lecture in comparison with the fierce humor of his adaptation of the Karaghiozis tradition. Only Rialdi, in her *Concentration Camp City*, remained faithful to her previous themes and techniques, even though the political and sexual humor is more explicit. That the anti-fascist repertoire lost its appeal in Greece after the restoration of democratic freedoms is only reasonable. There were complaints that the audience deserted the theater for television and other lesser forms of entertainment, but it seems more likely that, in their rush to return to the older, more realistic and openly political forms of drama which they had written before 1967, Greek playwrights, having failed to learn from their success with the abstract, indirect forms of theater with which they so profoundly touched their audiences, strayed from their audiences.

What are the conclusions one can draw from this account of the development of the theater in the time of tyranny? One can say the theater was forced by the constraints of censorship to seek new ways of communicating with audiences. In the resultant outpouring of new plays, playwrights realized that, not only were they capable of creating compelling drama despite the limitations imposed on them, but that the situation created large audiences capable of appreciating and eager for what they produced. What have we learned about the nature of theater, of its healing properties, in the laboratory of tyranny? Do these metaphysical plays have a role outside of the exceptional circumstances discussed in this chapter? We have seen that a theater of healing is more than just a subject for theoretical speculation. What took place was an unwanted and unexpected experiment in the effectiveness of different kinds of theatrical forms. In a situation where people needed more than mere diversion, the theater demonstrated that it can provide a forum where the unconscious mind reveals itself to the conscious mind bringing about an alleviation of suffering and an integration of body and mind. Furthermore, the communal experience of the theater showed that, as individuals came to terms with themselves, they were also able to overcome their isolation and alienation from society. In less than exceptional circumstances we cannot expect to find audiences so united in their distress, but there is little doubt that in each performance of a play there are individuals who experience its cathartic effect and find their lives transformed.

Chapter Five

Ionesco and the Journey of the Shaman

The ecstatic experience, the quest for which Ionesco shares with the shaman, is a means of breaking the grip of death over life, the restoration of the spectator's ability to experience life in its original state with all its freshness. Following in the footsteps of Artaud, Ionesco spent a lifetime seeking, in his dreams and waking experiences, the archetypal elements of a theatrical language capable of making metaphysical statements about human existence. Ionesco's recasting of his own experiences in terms of archetypal images for the theater, a movement from the particular to the universal, resembles the function of the shaman who acts as an intermediary between his people and the metaphysical realm beyond their reach. In a quarter-century of gradually re-working and clarifying what was once the dramatic representation of his personal experience and his dreams, Ionesco shaped his plays into ritual enactments of the voyage of the shaman. At the heart of his plays is the conflict between life and death, *eros* and *thanatos*; all else emanates from here: flight, entrapment, the lost paradise, obstacles and monsters. Whether it surfaces in the guise of the pursuit of an ideal woman or worlds of light and harmony, *eros* underlies humanity's unquenchable desire for the unattainable. Indeed the recuperation of each person's *eros* is the primary objective of the shamanic voyage. The triumph of *eros* is manifested by the ability to fly, one of the most characteristic of the shaman's powers. Flight symbolizes ecstasy, the ability of the soul to transcend the flesh (Eliade 479-480).

Although they appear in his plays in their twentieth-century manifestations, the motifs themselves are not unique to Ionesco; they are universal properties shared with, among others, the ecstatic trance of the shaman. In fact, there are so many similarities, it is possible to say that Ionesco is a contemporary shaman. The shaman is a champion of the forces of life over death, a role that Ionesco always claimed as his own. Ionesco's last and most shamanic plays, *Man with Bags* and *Voyages among the Dead*, recapitulate the themes and images of the plays that precede them and take a new step in showing the way to the victorious, ecstatic experience of life. Ionesco, like the shaman, sought to re-establish the primacy of life by making the spectator encounter death and the forms in which it manifests itself in life; to involve the spectator, in what Elizabeth Wright calls "death as a felt experience" (436). Both Ionesco and the shaman fight on behalf of life: the artist having assumed the functions once reserved to the tribal religious leader. Although, to my knowledge, Ionesco never referred directly to shamanism, it is clear that the playwright restored to the theater the archetypal motifs once performed for his people by one of the earliest people of the theater, the shaman.

According to Mircea Eliade, one of Ionesco's close friends and an advisor on matters related to myth (Bonnefoy 33), shamanism is primarily a technique of ecstasy. For the shaman the solutions to the problems of this world can be found only by exploring other-worldly, metaphysical domains while in an ecstatic trance. During the trance, the shaman's body remains on earth while the soul seeks out and struggles with the incorporeal foes of health and life, overcomes them and returns to earth to transmit the secret of this victory. The shaman "defends life, health, fertility, the world of 'light,' against diseases, sterility, disaster, and the world of 'darkness.'" Having undergone the ecstatic experience, the shaman, consequently, must find a way to make its content and meaning accessible to those who remained behind (511).

In addition to being a priest, mystic and poet, the shaman is a "psychopomp," i.e., he recreates the spiritual itinerary of the trance and leads others through it. The method is dramatic. The representation of the voyage of the shaman's soul is a staged, theatrical production (Eliade 508). The kind of staging varies from shaman to shaman, but the quality of the experience is the same and this is what concerns us insofar as it is related to Ionesco's plays (Charles 122). Having learned to escape the limited physical plane of human existence, the shaman can experience magical flight, or move by physical means—"rainbow, bridge, stairs, ladder . . . mountain"— from one plane to another. The shaman visits the underworld, paradise, and the past and explores the future while in the ecstatic trance. Evil and death become less frightening and inhibiting when described in the context of the shamanic voyage because they are thus placed in a more familiar, more human, context (Eliade 508).

It is difficult to imagine the repercussions of such a *spectacle* in a "primitive" community. The shamanic "miracles" not only confirm and reinforce the patterns of the traditional religion, but they also feed and stimulate the imagination, demolish the barriers between dream and present reality, open windows upon worlds inhabited by the gods, the dead, and the spirits (Eliade 511).

In a manner remarkably like that of the shaman, Ionesco selected and dramatized his experiences with the objective of giving the spectator the ability to experience life in all its freshness. As Ionesco defines it, ecstasy is the ability to experience life in all its freshness. Ionesco's expectations of the audience, although described in terms uniquely his, were not new, but something he shared with the other playwrights discussed in this book. To achieve such a metaphysical experience in the theater, the spectator must overcome what Viktor Shklovsky (whose theories influenced Brecht) called the "automatism of perception" and replace it with the direct experience of the world (qtd. in Jauss 85). Most people are incapable of ecstasy, according to Ionesco, because the fear of death makes each individual succumb to forces which turn existence into a living death. Encrusted in the familiar, in their habits, such persons lose their vitality. Their language consists of slogans and clichés; it exists autonomously, without thought. They become cogs in the machinery of mass society. Ionesco's objective is to help spectators escape this metaphysical predicament by means of a salutary confrontation with death. To do this he created a uniquely dramatic language which shuns normal verbal forms of communication in favor of an archetypal (hieroglyphic, Artaud might have added) language which speaks directly to the inner self by way of the emotions. It is a language which lies somewhere between the word and music. It permits him, as Ionesco says : "to reify anguish, internal presences" (NCN 63).

    Like the shaman, Ionesco was an opponent of the demonic in everyday life. He sought to protect the spectator from the power of the demonic (the unconscious powers which may contaminate the life bearing potential) by revealing and making familiar its nature. "To become conscious of the absurdity of the everyday and of language, of its improbability, is to have gone beyond it at the same time" (NCN 283). Shamanic drama achieves a similar end:

> The unknown and terrifying world of death assumes form, is organized in accordance with particular patterns; it finally displays a structure and, in the course of time, becomes familiar and acceptable. In turn the supernatural inhabitants of the world of death become *visible*; they show a form, display a personality, even a biography. (Eliade 492)

Ionesco gave concrete expression to inner feelings, the spoken or the unspeakable, those human experiences which do not possess a visible substance of their own: "of monstrous things, or monstrous conditions, without form, or of monstrous forms which we carry within us." (NCN 254). Ionesco sought in his dreams, as well as his waking experiences, images shared with all mankind. On this common experience, he imposed the form of a spiritual journey like that of the shaman.

Ionesco's archetypes (obstacles, monsters, entrapment, flight, the struggle between *eros* and *thanatos*) exist in embryonic form in his first plays where they are subsumed by his brilliant manipulation of language. The empty existence of Ionesco's characters and the absurdity of their world are veiled from their conscious minds by the automatic forms of communication which give the impression of life and thought where, in fact, there is only death. Ionesco smashed the façade, pushing his audience, if not his characters, toward a confrontation with the primary concerns of myth: love, life, death, struggle and suffering. Amid the meaningless chatter of the Smiths and the Martins, one can discern the prototypes of the sterile marriages which repress the vital libidinal impulses of his protagonists. The concurrently hilarious and disturbing flood of clichés, senseless explanations and *non sequiturs* of his early plays anticipate Ionesco's later attacks on ideological, scientific and demagogic cant. The human automatons in thrall to language are the precursors of the diverse cosmos of dehumanized beings to come. What is missing in the first plays is the hint that the absurdity of life can be challenged, that the alienation from the world can be overcome— at least on-stage.

The modern world is rife with monsters and ogres. Obviously, the playwright was not thinking of misshapen freaks with a green, scale-covered epidermis and bad teeth, but of normal-looking people with a horror within. The prototype of the Ionescan monster is more likely to be the person next door or ourselves:

> the man of received wisdom, of slogans, the conformism present everywhere . . . betrayed by his automatic language . . . talking without saying anything, talking because he has nothing personal to say, and the absence of life, the mechanism of the everyday" (NCN 253).

In dealing with the alienation and psychosis of ordinary life, Ionesco has chosen the same point of departure as the shaman.

The shaman works within a tradition of myth and ritual which specifies both the means and the ends of the ecstatic experience. The shaman's objective is to establish communication with the paradisiacal world of pre-lapsarian humanity where the secrets of a healthy, authentic existence can be found. In order to reach the other world, the shaman must master the secret of the "break-through in plane" which will permit the completion of a "perilous passage" in spite of mortal confrontations with variety of monsters and obstacles representing humanity's spiritual ills. In Ionesco's case, each new play was a measure of his development as a shaman— from his first plays, where he was clearly a novice, to *Man with Bags*, for example, where the First Man, his shamanic persona, completed all the steps of the shamanic voyage.

It is easier and more direct to demonstrate the emergence of the shamanic qualities of Ionesco's plays from the perspective of his later work, where they are clearly manifested, than to follow their chronological development. It is important to remember that Ionesco was not trying to tell a story, but to involve the spectator in a confrontation with death and neurotic manifestations of the fear of death. Even if the plots of some of his later plays seem conventional, it should be remembered that they exist only as a framework which permits Ionesco to display his archetypal images. By giving his plays a dreamlike atmosphere and by using language which is, as Dorothy Knowles describes it, "a form of behavior and not . . . a means of expression," Ionesco has attempted to force the spectator, who is accustomed to plays whose development is linear and whose language is literary, to perceive his plays differently, emotionally (436).

What did Ionesco want us to see and feel when he revealed the secrets of his vision of the world? For the shaman, there is an alternative to this fallen world. It is a lost paradise accessible to everyone before the fall, but which can now be visited only by means of the ecstatic trance (Eliade 265). Ionesco's lost world is much nearer. It is a vision, like Nietzsche's before him, of a lost childhood paradise; it is the memory of La Chapelle-Athenaise, where he spent "days of fullness, happiness and sunlight." For a child there is no distinction between the ecstatic experience of reality and "normal" perception. At some point, perhaps with the realization that we must all eventually die, the child forsakes the ability to perceive the world ecstatically and becomes an adult, a fallen creature. Familiarity with the world, says Ionesco, is the "original sin, . . . a slackening of attention, . . . it's losing the faculty of wonderment; oblivion; the paralysis bred by habit" (Bonnefoy 30, 31). Ionesco sought to restore the spectator's lost vision and thereby bring about a form of metaphysical salvation.

I have no evidence as to what Ionesco learned from Carl J. Jung when he underwent psychoanalysis with him, but whatever it was it must have reinforced and clarified the playwright's own instincts. Jung argued that there exists "a sphere of unconscious mythology whose primordial images are the common heritages of mankind." He felt that great art drew archetypal images from this "collective unconscious" thereby evoking "in us all those beneficent forces that . . . have enabled humanity to find a refuge from every peril and to outlive the longest night" (*Spirit* 80-82). In *The Undiscovered Self* Jung maintained that we must "remold these archetypal forms into ideas which are adequate to the challenge of the present" (82). In Jung's theories, Ionesco would certainly have found reassurance that bringing ancient shamanic motifs to the contemporary audiences was justified as a desperately needed contribution to its spiritual health.

When Ionesco's characters become aware enough to recognize their discontent with the *status quo* and articulate enough to explain it, they make it clear that they, like the shaman, are seeking to regain a lost paradise. However, until the First Man, Ionesco's characters are, at best, only novices doomed to fail despite the powerful inner vision that spurs them on. The Old Man in *The Chairs* yearns to see "The boats on the water making specks in the sunlight" (I. 131). The Old Man does no more than voice his desire and, reminded by his wife that such a sight is impossible because it is night, he subsides. Unwilling to resign themselves to the eternal darkness of a conventional life, Ionesco's later protagonists actively pursue their inner light even if it means giving up everything they possess.

In *The Killer* the memory of "that luminous moment which permitted me to put up with everything, which should have been my reason for existence, my support," sustains Bérenger as he works his way, obstacle after obstacle, to the *radiant city*. "You have restored to me my forgotten light," he says, giving premature thanks to the Architect (I. 80). Frustrated in his search for the way home, the First Man actually begins asking directions to La Chapelle-Anthenaise (Homme 61). *Man with Bags* contains the only successful attempt to recapture those lost moments of luminosity, although the First Man quickly realizes that it is not enough to ask directions and that the way is filled with the menace of failure. In a way, the growing sense of direction and confidence of each succeeding protagonist reflects Ionesco's own progress in identifying the archetypal elements of his theater.

From the perspective of Ionesco's more complex protagonists, it is possible to look back at the characters of the Professor, Jacques and the Old Couple to recognize the signs of incipient revolt. The decision to break out requires great courage and failure results in despair and regret. In *Thirst and Hunger*, when Jean, who has left home in search of his ideal woman, realizes that he will never find her, he regrets giving up the cocoon-like shelter of his pre-escape self "where I was walled in by my fear of death" (IV. 117). For others, the wall is a challenge which hides behind it the promise of renewal and salvation. In *The Stroller in the Air*, it is suggested that beyond the wall, "at once invisible and not transparent," there is an "anti-world" (III. 145). The recognition that the wall exists sets the protagonist apart from the others, because it entails the realization that, beyond the confines of this world, there is another, complementary world to be explored. To safely complete the perilous passage is to release oneself from the bonds of everyday reality.

As Ionesco's characters approach the "break-through in plane," they must surmount one final obstacle, usually a wall. The product of past fears and frustrations, the wall in Ionesco's plays symbolizes the spiritual condition of the protagonist and, in most cases, prevents him from going any further. In the world of the shaman a novice lacks the experience to complete the "perilous passage" safely (Eliade 485). To succeed one must have learned how to escape the flesh and become spirit. In this regard, all of Ionesco's protagonists, save the First Man and Jean in *Voyages*, can be considered novices who unwittingly place themselves in mortal peril.

Escape requires the ability to fly, one of the shaman's most characteristic powers. According to Eliade "magical flight is the expression both of the soul's autonomy and of ecstasy." The motifs of flight are an integral part of the shamanistic practice, although, as age-old expressions of the desire to imitate the flight of a bird or to dissociate the human soul from the body, they precede shamanism (Eliade 479-480). The ability to fly is proof that both the shaman and Ionesco's protagonist have transcended the limitations of a fallen humanity. As Bérenger, in *The Stroller in the Air*, says: "You are unhappy without knowing it. Because human misery comes from that; from the inability to fly, from having forgotten how" (III. 166).

Would it be far from the mark to ask if the power of Ionesco's early plays grows out of the the spectator's frustrated desire to see those absurd automatons break their bonds and fly? The evolution of Ionesco's protagonists from soulless puppets into shamanic characters is inspired by an almost imperceptible, but compelling need to make the world less menacing and alienating. To this end, Ionesco created an elemental protagonist, usually identified with the name Bérenger, whom Rosette Lamont describes as "visceral man stripped bare of his epidermis, quivering before our eyes" (1973: 210). Ionesco's Everyman has predecessors in Choubert and Amédée and successors in Jean, The Personage and the First Man. The generic, rather than the specific, names of his most later protagonists reinforce the impression that Ionesco's objective was to create archetypal characters for whom even the name, Bérenger, is too easily identifiable with a single individual.

Ionesco's protagonists deal with even the most mundane experience as though it were new and unique. They see life with an intensity beyond the ability of the average person. The First Man, for example, takes what he considers to be real risks. "All alone, I put myself in the mouth of the wolf. In the devil's lair. In the belly of the whale. At the doors of hell itself" (*Homme* 48). However, what the First Man perceives as a mortal danger is, for those around him, only a tourist attraction. That he can successfully undertake dangerous risks suggests that the First Man possesses special powers associated with the shaman for whom the myth of passing "though the jaws of a monster— is always a symbolic formula for 'intelligence,' 'wisdom,' 'transcendence,' and, in the last analysis, for initiation" (Eliade 485).

Ionesco's protagonist is a surrogate shaman who guides the spectator on a metaphysical voyage into realms of light and darkness, an experience of weightlessness and flight and of heaviness and forced descent. Like the shaman, he struggles to escape entrapment and to surmount obstacles such as human automatons, walls, mountains and, most dangerous of all, manifestations "of anguish, of inner presences" (NCN 63). These images arouse, as Paul Vernois pointed out, a nightmarish sense of "life caught in a snare" (76). The heaviness and forced descent are, according to Ionesco, intended to be concrete expressions of "totalitarianism, collectivism, the crowd, the mass." Together, the archetypal images constitute a dreamlike dramatization of "an imbalance between heaven and earth, a lack of synthesis, of integration" (Bonnefoy 36, 37).

While the shaman encounters obstacles recalling his natural, more primitive environment, the inner obstacles with which Ionesco's protagonists must deal manifest themselves in shapes which reflect the realities of our urbanized, technological civilization. In *The Chairs* the old couple's solitude and the Creator's inability to communicate have a physical correlative in the stage filled with empty chairs. In *Rhinoceros* those who surrender their humanity to the seductions of ideological conformity become an army of rhinoceroses rampaging through an office building and besieging Bérenger, the only one to resist. The proliferation of material objects is carried furthest in *The New Tenant* in which movers fill the stage to overflowing with furniture and then announce that there is more in the hallways, the streets and in the countryside beyond the city limits. In *Victims of Duty* Madelaine carries countless empty coffee-cups on-stage in thoughtless dutifulness, while her husband, Choubert, is obliged to stuff down dry bread, to weigh down his rebellious spirit.

The ultimate image of encirclement is conjured up poetically in *Exit the King* where the entire universe, paralleling his movement to death, closes in on King Bérenger. The First Man is surrounded, at different times, by soldiers who turn their bayonets on him and by two motorcyclists who enclose him within a ring of steel and flesh.

The setting of Ionesco's plays, a counterpart of the world visited by the shaman in his trance, completes the sense of isolation and encirclement. The old couple's lighthouse home is surrounded by water which, in the end, swallows up all evidence of their joint suicide. The *radiant city* of *The Killer*, with all of its edenic promise, serves only as a deadly mirage to lure Bérenger to his final confrontation with death. Ionesco's protagonists often find themselves entrapped, beguiled by a mirage like that of the *radiant city* which seems to materialize out of their own overpowering desire to regain a paradisiacal existence no more substantial than a vaguely recalled memory.

Choubert, Amédée, several of the Bérengers and Jeans undergo the ecstatic experience of luminosity and flight. Unfortunately for them, the moments of joy are of brief duration. Invariably they return to their former unhappy states where the principal images are of falling, of being sucked into a primal slough of anguish and hopelessness. Compare the above to an example cited by Eliade: "In New Zealand the deceased must pass through a very narrow space between two demons that try to capture him; if he is 'light' he gets through, but if he is 'heavy' he falls and becomes the demon's prey" (485).

In *Victims of Duty* an attempt at flight is aborted, because Choubert is literally incapable of the separating body from spirit. Although his spirit is carried higher into the heavens, his earth-bound body can go no higher than a chair placed on a table. His wife and the Policeman, playing the role of demons, capture him. The policeman force-feeds him bread in order to weigh him down (I. 227f). Like Choubert, Jacques is forced to stifle his instinct for life by declaring that he likes "pommes de terre au lard" (I. 104-105). In Ionesco's cosmos a poetic image of surrender is as "heavy" as all of the New Tenant's material possessions. In this world, death is not a question of one's physical condition, but of one's metaphysical state.

"The shaman has been able to contribute decisively to the *knowledge of death*," says Eliade (509). Ionesco sought to bring similar knowledge to his contemporaries. His plays are created with the object of breaking the grip of death on life. He sought to remind us, and himself, of what is easily forgotten, ignored or even hidden: "that truth about which we don't think and which is infinitely banal: I die, you die, he dies" (NCN 66). Human solidarity and the love of life can be regenerated only through communication which is genuine and direct. By reducing dead language, ideological cant and the materialistic sham of science and progress to litter on the stage, Ionesco attempted to clear the way for genuine communication. By means of a shamanistic confrontation with human mortality, Ionesco created an emotional awareness of the meaning and quality of death in our time and, as a consequence, an opportunity for the desire for life to reassert itself. "Without crisis," wrote Ionesco, "without the threat of death, there is nothing but death" (NCN 313).

Bérenger's showdown with death in *The Killer* is one of Ionesco's most powerful scenes. In this, the final scene of the play, Bérenger, attempting desperately to save his life, delivers a monologue enumerating various human responses to death. The Killer's only response is an occasional sardonic laugh. Having exhausted all of his arguments, Bérenger pulls out two pistols and threatens the Killer until he realizes that he lacks the will to shoot. "My strength is helpless against your cold determination, against your merciless cruelty! What can these bullets do against the infinite energy of your persistence?" (II. 171). Bérenger kneels, drops his pistols and accepts his fate. Death claims another victim, but, by the time the curtain falls, the spectator has been charged with a renewed sense of life. Bérenger, as Ionesco's *alter ego*, makes us confront death with him, thus performing the duty of the shaman.

The explosive charge which shatters the hold of death is primed by libidinal forces which escape every effort to curtail or manipulate them. While death may gain the upper hand on the stage, its power over the spectator is exorcised, because Ionesco's plays are charged with the power of creativity, love, idealism, desire, life: a "constructive and creative *eros*," according to Vernois (59). Manifested by the pursuit of ideal love and ideal worlds of light and harmony, *eros* is an abstract primal urge which transforms each person's eternal dissatisfaction with the mundane into a quest for the unattainable.[6] It underlies the shamanic idea of

---

[6] "Undergoing Jungian psychoanalysis in a Swiss nursing home, . . . [Ionesco] began to explore the connections between Buddhism and Freudianism, discovering in both the "awareness that *Eros*, or Desire, keeps us alive" (Lamont, *Macbeth* 248).

the lost paradise and the recuperation of *eros* as the objective of the shamanic voyage.

Socially determined, therefore unauthentic, expressions of love— love for one's parents or children, marriage, procreation and their more abstract forms such as duty, patriotism, and party loyalty— are evidence that we live in a fallen world. They are expressions of love subverted and an acceptance of the forces which draw people down and turn them into monsters. Married couples for whom love is an unknown or forgotten passion are in Ionesco's plays representative of the loss of *eros*. In the case of the Smiths and the Martins, the absence of love is evident in their total inability to communicate; they are drawn together not by a mutual passion, but simply because they are random beings fulfilling a proper social function and nothing more. In most cases the physical counterpart of the unhappy marriage is a deceptively peaceful domestic setting such as the Smith's living room, the apartments of Choubert and Amédée. Marie-Madelaine in *Thirst and Hunger* describes all of Ionesco's unhappy spouses when she comments on her husband Jean's constant dissatisfaction with his dwellings. "He thinks this house is like a tomb. Why does he work himself up like this? All houses are tombs" (IV. 97).

But the façade of propriety is everywhere subverted by libidinal undertones. In the later plays, the libidinal urge clearly drives the protagonist to set out in search of a lost world, happiness, life and ecstasy. The first plays only hint at the power of *eros*. For example, the abuse of the student by the Professor in *The Lesson* and her subsequent murder by him is dominated by a sense of overpowering desire and sexual violation. Jacques' family struggles to redirect the disobedient son's erotic energy into conventional forms such as marriage and procreation. The old couple, forgetting decorum, often disturb our sense of propriety with almost shocking expressions of suppressed sexual urges.

In *Victims of Duty* Madelaine's response to the Policeman, although indirect, is definitely sexual. Obviously aroused by the Policeman's display of authority and aggressiveness, Madelaine leaves the stage to prepare coffee, but returns without it. Instead, she has changed into a low-cut dress. According to the stage directions: "*she is another; her voice is changed; she has become tender and melodious*" (I. 94). Madelaine expresses her sexual excitement by making erotic gestures to her husband, but the source of her provocative behavior is the Policeman with whom she allies herself against Choubert. Bérenger Roi is stripped of everything— his empire, physical strength and life— while the characters around him reflect aspects of his younger, more vital self. Marie, his young second wife, is as Lamont points out, "an extension of Bérenger's own senses; his youth, his sensuality, his *eros*" (*Mass. Rev.* 145). Only in the scene in *Man with Bags* where the Woman meets the First Man is there a sense of health and balance as well as the promise of fulfillment.

Ionesco's protagonists attempt to escape their unhappy marriages, or, if unmarried like the Personage, they avoid wedlock in the naive expectation that someday their dream of love can be realized. The way they describe their ideal love leaves no doubt that finding it is tantamount to returning to the lost paradise. While the reasons for the revolts of Jacques, Amédée and Choubert are as vague as their intentions, in the later plays both the grievances and the expectations of the protagonists are better defined. The Personage in *What a Bloody Circus!* rebuffs the advances of Agnès, because he prefers to sit on the sidelines of life rather than compromise his ideals by marrying, having children or working. He prefers to wait for Lucienne, whose name combines the pursuit of ideal love with its etymological reference to light and, by extension, the break-through of the shaman's flight; however, she never appears.

Jean deserts his wife in *Thirst and Hunger* to keep a *rendez-vous* with an ideal woman as insubstantial as Lucienne. He has lost her photo and cannot remember what she looks like, but in trying to recall her he makes us aware of his longing for her and the impossible perfection she represents: "What memory did she awaken in me, what lost nostalgia, what hidden desires, what forgotten necessity! She awakened me to myself, she is the absolute necessity" (IV. 117). The ideal woman is the key to the lost paradise of memory and to the art of ecstasy. However, both Jean and the Personnage are condemned to eternal dissatisfaction with flesh-and-blood women.

Finding the woman of their dreams would be equivalent to achieving a breakthrough to the realms of light where the spirit can soar, but waiting without end is just another form of entrapment. In contrast to his dreams of escape, Agnès sees in Jean's waiting yet another form of death, of self-imprisonment. "While waiting you shut yourself in and you shut me in with you. . . . And you add shutter to shutter, you add walls to the walls that already exist" (IV. 116).

In the penultimate scene of *Man with Bags*, the First Man finally meets the woman all of Ionesco's protagonists have so ardently sought. She too has been waiting. "I came immediately after you left, in the hope that you would pass. I waited for you." For the first time in Ionesco's plays, the efficacious powers of love seem to be within grasp, the perilous passage has been completed:

> The waters will become clear, the sky transparent, people will no longer turn away when you pass, they will bless you and I shall be with you. I love you. . . . You'll see, tomorrow, everything will be new. (*Homme* 186)

The First Man has not escaped to another universe. Like the shaman, he has completed the ecstatic journey through the mystical domains of his psyche and has returned to the world from which he started. The woman who meets him is none other than the person who, in scene IV, identified herself as his wife. Everything is the same and yet everything has been transformed, because the First Man, having gained mastery over the shamanic technique of ecstasy, has been reconciled to his mortal human nature. Everything is new because he has acquired a new way of seeing the world. As Ionesco has said, "the world is at once marvelous and atrocious, a miracle and hell, and these antithetical feelings, the two obvious truths, constitute the backdrop of my personal existence and my oeuvre" (*Faces* 13). It is the recognition of the above duality which permits the First Man to reconcile himself to his wife and to rediscover the world as though he were present at the creation. The First Man becomes Adam, the first man, and with his Eve, he is prepared for life and for the recreation of mankind.

Voyages, one of Ionesco's last plays, demonstrates his virtuoso use of archetypal language. In his mature plays, those preceding *Voyages*, Ionesco organized his archetypal images and situations in linear fashion, rather like a conventional plot. In these plays the protagonist breaks out of the shell of everyday life and journeys past obstacles and monsters (reifications of his spiritual problems) in search of ideal worlds of light and beauty, and, only in *Man With Bags*, which precedes *Voyages*, does the protagonist actually complete the difficult passage. In *Voyages* we return to the non-linear organization of the first plays, but in a more complex form in which the opacity of the first plays alternates with the moments of absolute clarity of the later ones.

Jean wanders in the nightmarish world of the present, a world he would flee if only he possessed the strength and knowledge to do so. The means of escape is contained in the mystery of the dream language which he has forgotten; it is the source of the ecstatic vision. Feelings of guilt towards his parents and friends weigh him down and prevent him from gaining access to the world of light he seeks. The most insistent, recurring motif is Jean's anguished search for his mother whom he has not seen since he was a child and his father divorced her. Unlike the earlier plays with their comparatively simple plots involving obstacles and monsters which finally lead Ionesco's protagonists to the supreme test, the difficult passage, in *Voyages* there is instead a proliferation of images and situations presented in non-linear fashion and with an intensity that increases with each act. As Ionesco himself makes clear in the titles of the last two of three acts, the last two acts contain "themes and variations" of the first one. What remain constant are the archetypal elements of the shamanic voyage which appear not just once in this play, but repeatedly under many guises. Thus, with *Voyages*, Ionesco moved even further from the structure of the conventional play and toward his ideal: "a construction, composed of a series of states of consciousness, or of situations which intensify, become dense, then become tied together, either to become unraveled, or to end up both inextricable and intolerable" (NCN 329).

"I'd like to begin again," says Jean, provided everything were new" (III. 46). He longs to rediscover the time when he lived "passionately, That time was full, taut, rich. Things happened. Now . . . time is empty, slack, time flies. I can no longer grasp the instants, "the freshness of the first morning" (III. 43), and "the lost space" (III. 49).

Light, cities filled with light, a place where the spirit can soar: this is the lost paradise which fills every Ionescan protagonist with longing and dissatisfaction. Lydia reminds Jean of Aluminia, the city of light: "full of light. What light it was! A light different from light. And then we'd climb the side way up high . . . we'd arrive in the city of light" (III. 39).[7] In Act One, Jean relates his wanderings in search of "villes inattendues" and of an especially beautiful one whose name and location have slipped his mind. His father suggests it might have been Bocal, the capital of an ancient French colony in China. Jean cannot be sure; all he remembers is that the city's streets sloped down to the sea, like those of San Francisco. While father and son converse, the stage

---

[7] Eliade, commenting on the mystical experience of light in Ionesco's plays, draws our attention to their sources in the mysticism of the Eastern Orthodox Church: "Indeed for him, 'la lumière, c'est le monde transfiguré.' Such an expression brings to mind the idiom of the Byzantine mystics, particularly the Hesychasts and Gregory Palamas in discussing the Light of the Transfiguration on Mount Tabor. But for Eugène Ionesco this 'miracle' is part of our world . . ." (*Faces* 23-24).

directions call for the projection of images of a huge river, lush vegetation and light-filled trees (5-6).

When Jean speculates about metaphysical realms, he is indulging in an exercise typical of Ionesco's protagonists. "Maybe there are overlapping spaces one within the other, separated by imaginary curtains, by partitions. Maybe there are times within the same time at once one and separate" (III. 42-43). For Jean (as well as for Ionesco) one key to these other realms is the language of the dream. Jean assures Lydia that he can find Aluminia because "it's marked on all dream maps" (III. 39).

Ionesco's idea of the monstrous, of being a monster, is the substitution of habit for the vital life. A monster is a person whose fear of death has cut him off from the vision of the city of light. To be a monster is to function like a machine according to prevailing cultural and political norms, without feeling, unauthentically. Jean experiences the monstrous with varying degrees of intensity. At times he is its passive thrall. At others, he represents the human spirit fighting to liberate itself. Jean has been a typical Ionescan monster "enmeshed in things . . . the habitual having become habitual and abnormality having become the norm, I told myself that I was home after all" (II. 51).

Jean's smugness vanishes when the familiar, comfortable furniture around him suddenly is transformed into menacing, deadly creatures. "The chair was a two-headed dragon, the armoire something like a lake" (II. 51). For all of Ionesco's protagonists the conventional home is a cage, a prison or a tomb from which they must escape. We are given a clue to the character of Jean's mother when we are told that her favorite home is "a handsome black chateau" (I. 11) which resembles a casket. When Jean recognizes the true nature of the everyday world of habit in the transmogrified objects in his living room, there is a moment of illumination: he acquires the wisdom and intelligence given to the shaman as part of his initiation (Eliade 485).

Knowledge of the true nature of the world is not enough to make one a full-fledged shaman; on Jean it confers only novice status and all the accompanying dangers. Mortal peril is inevitable for if one insists on living life to its fullest, it must be with a concomitant willingness to face death. Jean's case is unique in that he experiences both failure and success frequently whereby Ionesco implies that the ecstatic vision must constantly be renewed and protected from the encroachment of death.

The hold of death is broken by libidinal forces which defeat every effort to curtail or manipulate them. Even when Jean seems to succumb momentarily to the power of death (expressed in images of heaviness, descent, darkness, guilt), its hold over the spectator is exorcised by the power of *eros*.

Preceding take off many of Ionesco's protagonists actually do soar or, at least, approach take off before they come crashing down. Like his predecessors, Jean encounters many obstacles which impede his escape. The obstacles in Jean's path are reifications of his spiritual problems. On his way to visit his grand-father and other relatives, in the world of the dead, Jean explains, "I traversed paths of mud" (I. 2). To visit other worlds, the Shaman must become pure spirit; mud symbolizes Jean's remaining ties to the earth. Later, Arlette compares the guilt which restrains Jean from crossing the threshold of the other world to mud. "Bury yourself in the mud of your guilt" (III. 44).

The paralyzing effect of this guilt is demonstrated in the scene of temptation which follows. Arlette removes her dress and stands before him naked, a living symbol of *eros*, of liberation. Jean cannot move because he feels responsible for the death of Alexandre, once his rival for Arlette. Even the appearance of Alexandre, who forgives Jean and asks him, as a friend, to take Arlette, is not enough to lift the burden. Jean remains immobilized—"I didn't dare. I stood there nailed to the spot" (III. 45). Taking that first step toward Arlette would be equivalent to beginning the dangerous passage of the shaman. "I should have crossed the threshold, jumped over the wall. I couldn't make up my mind to do it" (III. 46).

Jean's incapacitating burden of guilt is compounded by failures past and present. His feelings toward his father are a mixture of hate and, if not necessarily love, sympathy. There is hate because his father deserted his wife and robbed her of Jean and her other children. He despises the political opportunist and bureaucrat who pretends to be an artist. I have written a "*roman gris,*" the father boasts to Jean (I. 6). At the same time Jean feels guilty because he has not become the success his father wanted him to be. It is evident each man desires understanding and reconciliation, but they are separated by an insurmountable wall.

In Jean's mind the realm of lights, the ideal dwelling and the liberation of his creative powers are connected with finding his mother whom he has not seen since he was a child. Unfortunately, once he is in her presence he finds neither love nor warmth. The mother is an aged woman, hardly distinguishable from his grandmother. She welcomes him with a rebuke for taking so long to visit her (II. 60f). There is no love to be found in his family. Even Miss Simpson, his stepmother, is a child-hating martinet (II. 64).

Almost all of Ionesco's protagonists abandon home leaving their wives behind. In *Voyages* it is the father, not Jean, who abandons his wife. Moreover, he is unfaithful to the second wife. The father's constant search for the perfect woman is crowned by his affair with the Gypsy. The second wife, to whom he refers as "Hélène," "la Belle Hélène" (I. 7), is a case of mistaken identity: she is not Helen of Troy, merely Miss Simpson. Like Jean, the father is weighted down by guilt generated by the conflict between reality and his own search for the ideal. "Loaded down with work, crushed by guilt for I was not a brute, contrary to what you think, that [the love of the Gypsy woman] was the joy of my life. The only one" (I. 12).

Whereas the father returns from the dead to unburden himself, the mother's side of the family comes only to take revenge. The old woman, "at once grand-mother and grand-father," avenges the suffering of Jean's mother. The old woman attacks the step-mother, a cross between a sorceress and a whore in this scene, who turns into an old hump-backed woman. The old woman slaps around a bureaucrat (one of the father's inhuman functions), who collapses. She kills the Captain, the father's brother. The Gypsy strangles the father and drags him offstage with her. Having taken vengeance, the harridan is transformed into a beautiful young woman who "gives off cries of joy which, properly speaking, are inhuman" (III. 52-58). However, the slaughter of monsters, or of monstrous figures, does not clear the way for Jean to complete the dangerous passage, it only sets the stage for one final, intense reiteration of the archetypal symbols and situations of the shaman's itinerary.

Voyages ends ambiguously with hope and despair contending fiercely for control of Jean's spirit. "The opening is narrower than the valve on a tire," he complains (III. 60). Jean feels himself pulled in different directions. "They stretched your hands from one bridge to the other, they pulled your legs" (III. 61). Even his declining popularity as an artist is described in terms of forced descent.

But Jean knows that the passage, dangerous though it may be, is not impossible for him. Alexandre counsels Jean that it is possible to make the difficult passage: "There's an opening which you might find. Which I found once. But, in any case, you have to find it" (III. 47). Jean reports several successful passages, one, for example:

> I'd taken only one step, a door which wasn't visible opened. I traveled for hundreds of kilometers in the world, for thousands of kilometers, and now to get here, a door opened wide or rather I went through a window or a mirror. It all took place without my knowledge. And it's the greatest voyage. (II. 52)

The passage is repeated twice by Jean: once in an abstract, suggestive way similar to the one above (III. 60) and then, immediately afterward, in the context of the most prosaic biographical details (III. 61).

Whether Jean completes his voyage or not is immaterial, because Ionesco is not trying to tell a story. He is trying to bring about a change in the life of the spectator, to make sensible and comprehensible the absurdity of an existence controlled by the neurotic fear of death, to compel a liberating encounter with it. Like the shaman, he wants to cure spiritual ills and not merely to entertain. Ionesco knew, as we all do, that we cannot be reconciled to death, but we can learn to love life, to desire it enough to make it prevail over paralysis and death. He wants to make us agree with Jean that, despite all the evidence to the contrary, "It's good to be alive" (I. 20).

The absurdity of existence and our ultimate inability to know the truth are common themes of the literature of the West in the twentieth century. For many this awareness of our human condition has been a source of despair, but for Ionesco—and the others who see the theater as a source of metaphysical healing—this awareness is the first step in achieving spiritual health. In helping us shed the illusions of our time, the theater does not need to leave us empty; instead, as Ionesco has shown, it can remind us of the world, of its beauty, of what is authentic and true.

Chapter Six

Conclusion

We have been unrequited in our search for a theater that works magic, performs miracles, but what about the more serious question of metaphysical truth? What has been accomplished? For one, the search for a metaphysical drama provided a powerful impetus for experimentation with theatrical forms. In the process, the theater of the West, which developed almost as a footnote to Aristotle's *Poetics*, found itself free to assume almost any guise imaginable. Different, hitherto alien, forms of theater were examined on the principle that if something worked, it should be appropriated. The theater of the West, in its imperial ransacking of various non-Western forms of drama, became truly cosmopolitan. Eventually, the kind of theater Mallarmé could only dream of became a reality. The inventiveness shown by playwrights and theater groups has demonstrated the groundlessness of Nietzsche's fear that the cooperation between the apollonian and the dionysian would result in the later being squeezed out again. The old classics are still revived to play their older role, and realistic plays continue to predominate on the stage, but at the same time, we are offered a feast of constantly evolving and multiplying theatrical forms.

The role of metaphysical theater under conditions of tyranny seems indisputable. At the same time, it is here we realize that our personal reaction to a theatrical performance in more normal times is not necessarily an isolated occurrence. It is in this experience that we find the confidence to assert that the theater permits the subconscious mind to communicate with the conscious mind, that it can transform our hearts and minds.

Our subjective experience in the theater implants in our minds and hearts an image of what we sense to be true and gives it metaphysical expression. Long before Barthes' *Mythologies* provided us with a critique of the charter myths of our time, long before deconstructivist and semiological critics, the metaphysical playwrights, eschewing the jargon and opaque disquisitions of the critics, learned to separate sign from signifier in a moment of theatrical illumination which restores to the spectator the freedom of the imagination and the responsibility to make a personal determination of any new significance which must be ascribed to the sign. Their plays demonstrate the validity of Jauss's definition of catharsis as a preparation for intellectual change which begins during the performance and later finds its completion as we reflect on its significance (92).

Of the playwrights I have discussed, Ionesco was the most sceptical about what could be accomplished by the theater. Nevertheless, in an essay entitled "Why I Write," he made it clear that the mission of the theater was important, more than mere entertainment, and that if it provides only a fraction of what it sometimes promises, it remains essential:

> Our social awareness flows from our metaphysical consciousness, of our existential intuition. By not forgetting who we are, where we are at, we will understand ourselves better. A human fraternity based on the metaphysical condition is more secure than one grounded in politics. A questioning without a metaphysical answer is far more authentic, and in the end useful than all the false and partial answers given by politics. (14)

Works Cited

Abel, Lionel. *Metatheatre*. New York: Hill & Wang, 1963.

Aksyonov, Vasily. Lecture. *Eastern European Drama and the American Stage*. New York: Center for Advanced Study in Theatre Arts, 1984.: 19-26.

Albright, Daniel. "Pound , Yeats, and the Noh Theater." *Iowa Review* 15 (1985): 34-50.

Artaud, Antonin. *Oeuvres complètes*. Vols. IV-V. Poitiers: Gallimard, 1964. (Translations are mine.)

Balakian, Anna. *Surrealism: The Road to the Absolute*. New York: E. P. Dutton, 1970.

Barthes, Roland. "Le Balcon." *Théâtre populaire*. 38 (1960): 96-98.

Beaumont, Keith. *Alfred Jarry: A Critical and Biographical Study*. New York: St. Martin's, 1984.

Ben Jelloun, Tahar. "Un crépusculaire odeur l'isole." *Magazine littéraire*. September 1993: 29-32.

Berdyaev, Nicholas. *The Beginning and the End*. Trans. R. M. French. New York: Harper & Brothers, 1952.

---. *The Fate of Man in the Modern World*. Trans. Donald A. Lowrie. Ann Arbor: U Michigan P, 1961.

Bergson, Henri. *Le Rire*. Paris: P.U.F., 1940.

Bentley, Eric. *The Dramatic Event*. Boston: Beacon, 1954.

Block, Haskell M. *Mallarmé and the Symbolist Drama*. Detroit: Wayne State U., 1963.

Bonnefoy, Claude. *Conversations with Eugène Ionesco*. Trans. Ian Dawson. New York: Holt, Rinehart & Winston, 1970.

Brecht, Bertolt. *Brecht on Theatre*. Ed. and Trans. John Willett. New York: Hill and Wang, 1964.

---. *The Caucasian Chalk Circle*. Rev. Trans. and Intro. Eric Bentley. New York: Evergreen-Grove,1963.

---. *Galileo*. Trans. Charles Laughton. Intro. Eric Bentley. Evergreen-Grove, 1966.

---. *The Good Woman of Setzuan*. Rev. Trans. Eric Bentley. New York: Evergreen-Grove, 1961.

---. *Jungle of Cities*. Trans. Anselm Hollo. In *Jungle of Cities and Other Plays*. New York: Evergreen-Grove, 1966.

---. Program Notes. *Jungle of Cities*. ASTA Production, Washington, D. C. 24 March-24 April, 1977.

---. *The Measures Taken*. In *The Jewish Wife & Other Plays*. Trans. Eric Bentley. New York: Evergreen-Grove, 1965.

---. *Mother Courage*. Trans. and Intro. Eric Bentley. New York: Evergreen-Grove, 1966.

---. *Saint Joan of the Stockyards*. Trans. Frank Jones. Intro. Frederic Garb. Bloomington: Indiana UP, 1969.

Butcher, S. H., Trans. and Intro. *Aristotle's Theory of Poetry and Fine Art: With a Critical Text and Translation of The Poetics*. New York: Dover, 1951.

Calandra, Denis. "The Aesthetics of Reception and Theatre." *New Directions in Theatre*. Ed. Julian Hilton. Hong Kong: Macmillan, 1993. 13-24.

Campbell, Joseph. *The Hero with a Thousand Faces*. Princeton: Bollingen-Princeton UP, 1949.

Cassirer, Ernst. *Mythical Thought*. Trans. Ralph Manheim. New Haven: Yale UP, 1955. Vol. 2 of *The Philosophy of Symbolic Forms*. 3 vols.

Chapman, Wayne K. "*Symbolisme* and Its 'Chief' Agent in English: Mallarmé vis-à-vis Yeats." *Romance Quarterly* 37 (1990): 19-29.

Charles, Lucille Hoerr. "Drama in Shaman Exorcism." *Journal of American Folklore*. 66 (1953): 92-122.

Chtiguel, Olga F. "Without Theatre, the Czechoslovak Revolution Could Not Have Been Won." *The Drama Review* 34 (1990): 88-96.

Clogg, Richard. *A Concise History of Greece*. Cambridge: Cambridge UP, 1992.

Del Caro, Adrian. *Dionysian Aesthetics: The Role of Destruction and Creation as Reflected in the Life and Works of Friederich Nietzsche*. Frankfurt am Main: Peter D. Lang, 1981.

Eliade, Mircea. "Eugene Ionesco and 'La Nostalgie du Paradis'." Lamont. 1978. 21-30.

---. *Shamanism: Archaic Techniques of Ecstasy*. Rev. ed. Trans.Willard R. Trask. Princeton: Bollingen-Princeton UP, 1964.

Ellman, Richard. *Yeats-The Man and the Masks*. New York: Dutton, 1958.

Esslin, Martin. *Brecht: The Man and His Work*. Rev. ed. Garden City: Anchor-Doubleday, 1971.

---. *The Theatre of the Absurd*. Garden City: Anchor-Doubleday, 1961.

Fuegi, John. *Bertolt Brecht: Chaos, According to Plan*. Cambridge: Cambridge UP, 1987.

---. *The Essential Brecht*. Los Angeles: Hennesey & Ingals, 1972.

Genet, Jean. Interview. "Jean Genet:Affirmation of Existence Through Rebellion." By Rüdiger Wischenbart. *Journal of Palestinian Studies*. 16 (1987): 64-84.

---. *Le Balcon*. Décines: L'Arbalète, 1956. (Translations are mine.)

---. *Les Bonnes & Comment jouer les bonnes*. Décines: L'Arbalète, 1963. (all translations are mine.)

---. *Haute Surveillance*. Mayenne: Gallimard, 1965. (Translations are mine.)

---. *Les Nègres*. Décines: L'Arbalète, 1958. (Translations are mine.)

---. *Les Paravents*. Décines: Marc Barbezat, 1961. (Translations are mine.)

Gerould, Daniel. "Introduction." *Eastern European Drama and the American Stage*. New York: Center for Advanced Study in Theatre Arts, 1984. 1-7.

---. "Tyranny and Comedy." *Comedy: New Perspectives*. Ed. Maurice Charney. New York: New York Literary Forum, 1978. 3-30.

Gray, Ronald. *Brecht the Dramatist*. Cambridge: Cambridge UP, 1976.

Hofstadter, Albert. *Truth and Art*. n.p., Minerva, 1968.

Innes, Christopher. *Holy Theatre: Ritual and the Avant Garde*. Cambridge: Cambridge UP, 1981.

Ionesco, Eugène. *L'Homme aux valises suivi de Ce Formidable bordel!* Paris: Gallimard, 1975. (Translations are mine.)

---. "Ni un dieu, ni un démon," *Cahiers de la Compangie Madelaine Renaud–Jean-Louis Barrault* 9 (1957): 22-27. (Translations are mine.)

---. *Notes et contre-notes*. Saint-Amand: Idées-Gallimard, 1966. (Translations are mine.) All references to this source in the text appear as NCN.

---. *Théâtre*. 4 vols. Paris: Gallimard, I-1954, II-1958, III-1963, IV-1966. (Translations are mine.)

---. *Voyages chez les morts*, in *La Nouvelle revue française*, Act I, No. 324 (1 Jan., 1980); Act II, No. 325 (1 Feb., 1980); Act III, No. 326 (1 Mar., 1980).

---. "Why I Write." Trans. Rosette C. Lamont. Lamont. 1978. 14-20.

Jauss, Hans Robert. *Aesthetic Experience and Literary Hermeneutics*. Trans. Michael Shaw. Vol. 3 of *Theory and History of Literature*. Ed. Wlad Godzich and Jochen Schulte-Sasse. Minneapolis: U Minnesota P, 1982. 3 vols.

Jung, Carl Gustav. *The Spirit in Man, Art, and Literature*. Trans. R. F. C. Hull. Vol. 15 of *The Collected Works of C. G. Jung*. Eds. Herbert Read and others. Princeton: Princeton UP, 1966.

---. *The Undiscovered Self*. Trans. R. F. C. Hull. New York: Mentor, 1958..

Keene, Donald. *No: The Classical Theatre of Japan*. Tokyo: Kodansha, 1966.

Kitazawa, Masakuni. "Myth, Performance, and Politics." *The Drama Review* 36 (1992): 160-173.

Knapp, Bettina L. *Antonin Artaud: Man of Vision*. New York: Discus-Avon, 1969.

Knowles, Dorothy. "Ionesco and the Mechanisms of Language." *Modern Drama* 5 (1970): 7-10.

Laing, R. D. *Self and Others*. Baltimore: Penguin, 1969.

Lamont, Rosette C. and Melvin J. Friedman, eds. *The Two Faces of Ionesco*. Troy, NY: Whitston, 1978.

Lamont, Rosette C. "The Double Apprenticeship: Life and the Process of Dying." *The Phenomenon of Death: Faces of Mortality*. Ed. Edith Wyshogrod. New York: Harper & Row, 1973: 198-224.

---. An Interview with Eugène Ionesco." *The Massachusetts Review*. 10 (1969): 128-148.

---. "From *Macbeth* to *Macbett*," *Modern Drama* 15 (1972): 231-253.

---. "The Metaphysical Farce: Beckett and Ionesco." *French Review*. 32 (1959): 319-328.

Langer, Susan K. *Philosophy in a New Key*. 3rd. ed., rev. Cambridge: Harvard UP, 1957.

Mallarmé, Stéphane. *Oeuvres complètes*. Vols. IV-V. Ed. Henri Mondor and G. Jean-Aubry. Paris: Pléiade-Gallimard, 1945. (Translations are mine.)

May, Keith M. *Nietzsche and Modern Literature: Themes in Yeats, Rilke, Mann, and Lawrence*. New York: St. Martin's, 1988.

Memmi, Albert. *Portrait du colonisé précédé du Portrait du colonisateur*. Paris: Payot, 1973.

Metscher, T. W. H. "Brecht and Marxist Dialectics." *Oxford German Studies* 6 (1972): 132-144.

Nietzsche, Frederich. *The Birth of Tragedy and the Genealogy of Morals*. Trans. Francis Golffing. Garden City: Anchor-Doubleday, 1956.

Oslzly, Petr. "On Stage with the Velvet Revolution." *The Drama Review*. 34 (1990): 97-108.

Pound, Ezra and Ernest Fenollosa. *The Classic Noh Theater of Japan*. New York: New Directions, 1959.

Putzel, Steven. "Poetic Ritual and Audience Response: Yeats and the No." *Yeats and Postmodernism*. Ed. Leonard Orr. Syracuse: Syracuse UP, 1991: 105-125.

Rank, Otto. *The Myth of Birth of the Hero and Other Writings*. Ed. Philip Freund. New York: Vintage, 1964.

Rimbaud, Arthur. "Bad Blood." Trans. Bertrand Mathieu. *A Season in Hell*. Cambridge, MA: Pomegranate, 1976.

Rosemont, Franklin. *André Breton and the First Principles of Surrealism*. London: Pluto, 1978.

Sartre, Jean-Paul. *Un Théâtre de situations*. Ed. Michel Contat and Michel Rybalka. Saint-Amand: Idées-Gallimard, 1973. (Translation is mine.)

Seiden, Morton Irving. *William Butler Yeats: The Poet as a Mythmaker 1865-1939*. New York: Cooper Square, 1975.

Simon, Alfred. *Dictionnaire de théâtre français contemporain*. Paris: Larousse, 1970.

Sontag, Susan, ed. and intro. "Introduction." *Antonin Artaud: Selected Writings*. New York: Farrar, Straus and Giroux, 1976.

Speirs, Ronald. *Brecht's Early Plays*. Atlantic Highlands, NJ: Humanities, 1982.

Thiher, Allen. "Jacques Derrida's Reading of Artaud: 'La Parole soufflée' and 'La Clôture de la représentation'." 57 *French Review* (1984): 503-509.

Tucker, Robert. *Philisophy and Myth in Karl Marx*. New York: Cambridge UP, 1972.

Vernois, Paul. *La Dynamique théâtrale d'Eugène Ionesco*. Paris: Klincksieck, 1972. (Translations are mine.)

White, Edmund. *Genet*. London: Chatto & Windus, 1993.

Wirth, Andrzej. "Brecht and the Asiatic Model: The Secularization of Magical Rites." *Literature East & West*. 15 (1971): 601-615.

Wright, Elizabeth C. "The Vision of Death in Ionesco's *Exit the King*." *Soundings* 54 (1971): 435-449.

Wulbern, Julian H. *Brecht and Ionesco: Commitment in Context*. Urbana: U of Illinois P, 1971.

Yeats, William Butler. *The Autobiographies*. Garden City: Doubleday, 1958.

---. *Essays and Introductions*. New York: MacMillan, 1961 (referred to as EI).

Index